The WOMEN in the GOSPEL OF JOHN

The WOMEN in the GOSPEL OF JOHN

The Divine Feminine

Judith Kaye Jones

CHALICE
PRESS
ST. LOUIS, MISSOURI ·

Bible quotations, unless otherwise marked, are from the *New Revised Standard Version Bible,* copyright 1989, Division of Christian Education of the National Council of the Churches of Christ in the United States of America. Used by permission. All rights reserved.

Cover art: Copyright © 2004 by Judith Kaye Jones
Cover and interior design: Elizabeth Wright

Visit Chalice Press on the World Wide Web at
www.chalicepress.com

10 9 8 7 6 5 4 3 2 1   08 09 10 11 12

Library of Congress Cataloging–in–Publication Data

Jones, Judith Kaye.
   The women in the gospel of John : the divine feminine / by Judith Kaye Jones.
      p. cm.
   ISBN 978-0-8272-4257-9
   1. Bible. N.T. John—Criticism, interpretation, etc. 2. Women in the Bible. 3. Lent. 4. Worship programs. I. Title.

BS2615.52.J67 2008
226.5'0922082–dc22

2008023008

Contents

Preface   vii

Introduction   1

Chapter 1: New Wine   5

Chapter 2: Living Water   13

Chapter 3: New Law   23

Chapter 4: New Hope   33

Chapter 5: New Discipleship   43

Chapter 6: Another Beginning   49

Chapter 7: New Life   55

Conclusion   69

Appendix A: Seven-Week Study Guide   71

Appendix B: Worship Series: "Driving Away the Dark"   79

     1 Behold a Woman   80

     2 First Sunday in Lent: New Wine   81

     3 Second Sunday in Lent: Water That Is Alive   84

     4 Third Sunday in Lent: The Sound of Stones Falling   86

     5 Fourth Sunday in Lent: Rolling the Stone Away   89

     6 Fifth Sunday in Lent: The Fragrance of Faith   92

     7 Sixth Sunday in Lent: My Son, My Son   94

     8 Easter Sunday: Rabboni!   96

Appendix C: Art Installations for "Driving Away the Dark"   99

Appendix D: The Women's Tale (A Play)   103

Bibliography   119

Preface

Nearly thirty years ago I was a seminary student at Pacific School of Religion in Berkeley, and enrolled in a biblical studies course on the gospel of John. I had, because of the vision and forbearance of several of my professors, developed a habit of creating art projects to satisfy course requirements. Fascinated by Raymond Brown's article on women in the gospel of John,[1] I decided to explore the seven stories in both text and art. The result was a project of seven watercolors, with a dramatic monologue accompanying each one. As I studied the text I became more and more convinced that the stories of women were not just important to this gospel, but that they represented its major themes. They were, in effect, the gospel.

I continued to work with this material over the next decade, largely in workshops and Bible studies. At the Quadrennial Assembly of the Christian Women's Fellowship (CWF) of the Christian Church (Disciples of Christ) in the United States and Canada (CCDC) in 1990 at Purdue University, I presented a new set of drawings, and the material I had so far developed. I felt a shade of uneasiness, as, after all, there were women there from all over the United States, most of them far from Berkeley and the feminist theological community there. A woman from Kentucky, who was participating in the workshop, raised her hand when I asked for questions. With delight sparkling on her face, she asked, "Do you think it could have been written by a woman?" I shall never forget the thrill of both astonishment and recognition I felt in hearing that question. She had asked a most radical question, one I had asked in seminary and which had been received with polite tolerance. It went to the very heart of women in religious studies and in the church. Some ideas were just too radical to express: using feminine language for God, seeing women in leadership roles in the early church equal to men, and certainly, authorship of one of the canonical gospels.

After the publication of Dan Brown's novel *The Da Vinci Code,* popular culture suddenly became aware of some of these issues. The blockbuster best-seller did what Bible studies and the voices of women scholars and teachers had not been able to do. It posed difficult questions about the role of women in Jesus' life and in the early church and suggested some fascinating answers. This was both a bane and a blessing. It was a bane because, after all, it is a novel based largely upon legendary material, some totally false pseudo-documents, and a lively imagination. It is a fun read for those of us who love mysteries, but it is a *novel.* The amazing storm of controversy it provoked, however, made clear that many people are longing for new insights into what had become unquestioned role identification and limitation of women based on biblical accounts. Women, and men too, were suddenly outraged at the suggestion that women's voices had been suppressed, their stories erased, their influence denied. The divine feminine suddenly became not just a phrase used by radical feminist theologians and "Goddess" worshipers (who are, by the way, not invariably one and the same) but by people everywhere, churched and unchurched.

As frustrating as this novel's success may have been for serious students of the Bible and church history, it did open the door to popularizing more serious and significant studies of Mary Magdalene in particular, and women in the Bible and early church in general. Of the many fine works available, I recommend especially two: Karen King's *The Gospel of Mary of Magdala: Jesus and the First Woman Apostle,* and Sandra M. Schneiders' *Written That You May Believe: Encountering Jesus in the Fourth Gospel.* For a more extensive, but by no means exhaustive, list, see the Bibliography.

Notes

[1]Raymond E. Brown, "Roles of Women in the Fourth Gospel," App. 2 in *The Community of the Beloved Disciple: The Lives, Loves, and Hates of an Individual Church in New Testament Times* (New York: Paulist Press, 1979), 183–98.

Introduction

"In the beginning…" (Gen. 1:1; Jn. 1:1).

I looked up *mystery* in the very old dictionary that sits on my desk. It defined *mystery* as sacred secrets, particularly with regard to secret rites, and also the type of plays acted on the steps of the great cathedrals during the Middle Ages, designed to teach an illiterate population the stories and events of the Bible. Interestingly, it did not mention a story about a crime in which the entertainment factor came from trying to figure out "who done it."

Lots of us like to settle down in the evening, after a long day, with a good book. Some erudite souls read history or philosophy to relax. I knew someone like that once. Some of us read magazines for our houses, our bodies, our hobbies, or our hair. But others—and I would be willing to bet a good number, like nothing so much as to sink down in that easy chair beside the fire, or prop up on an extra pillow with quilt and cat, and lose ourselves in a good mystery. Whether you favor the gently horrifying mysteries of the classic English country house, such as those written by Dorothy Sayers and Agatha Christie, or prefer the more hard-boiled variety by Rex Stout or Raymond Chandler, there is something about a mystery that engages our imaginations in a way no other type of reading can do. Or maybe you are one of the millions who were fascinated (enraged, entertained?) by Dan Brown's *The Da Vinci Code*. I know there are plenty of mysteries on television to soothe the tired brain with who done it and why, but for sheer escapism, nothing beats a good mystery book that allows your mind to wander the moors with the heroine in search of strange noises, or sip tea while wondering who in the house poisoned the master of the mansion, or discover the body in the library. Why do we love a mystery?

Some of us actually read the Bible, which is the biggest, the greatest, mystery of all time. On the one hand, we have the fundamentalists who claim that it is the perfectly consistent, perfectly received text direct from the mind of God to the hand of man, immutable, unchangeable, and absolutely true. On the other hand, we have scholars studying and examining the text, line by line and word by word, noting shades of meaning, historical relationship and context, challenging the traditional understandings of stories and words spoken, challenging the meaning of miracles and messages, asking questions that probe the heart of the mystery and the souls of believers.

1

In 2004 American religious culture was under siege by two forms of popular entertainment: a novel and a movie. The novel, *The Da Vinci Code*, gathers up ideas and theories and legends that have been explored by both men and women scholars for years regarding the character and importance of Mary Magdalene. Drawing upon a variety of sources for stories and legends, Dan Brown has truly thrown the cat among the pigeons with his thriller involving the possible marriage and offspring of Jesus of Nazareth, and a plot by the church to lie to and defraud generations of faithful, believing Christians. The novel explores the deliberate eradication of the divine feminine from Scripture and tradition, silencing the voices of women and their experience as it related to the life of the one known as Jesus. The other, a movie made by Mel Gibson, portrays the Passion of Jesus, three hours of suffering and torture, emphasizing the centrality of the sacrifice of God's Son for the sake of humanity's salvation. Two extremes are posited. On one extreme, *The Da Vinci Code* presents a nondivine Jesus elevated to divinity by a power-hungry Emperor Constantine, seeking to consolidate his absolute power over his diverse empire. The novel's suggestion left millions of believing Christians angry and puzzled and asking, "Can that possibly be true?" The other extreme portrayed a supremely divine Jesus, God himself come down in human flesh, dying horribly—visually, twenty-feet long and twelve feet high in surround sound and living, bloody color—to save our souls, yours and mine.

The gospel of John presents us with the ultimate mystery—God with us—and the witnesses to the revelation of God's love. These witnesses who have, until fairly recent times, been silenced by prejudice and oppression, were the women who accompanied, who served, who loved Jesus; who were healed by him; who tended to him; and who stayed with him until the end, at the cross, at the tomb. Their voices then fall inexplicably silent, leaving us to wonder: What did they really see? What did they really hear and understand? Most poignant of all, What happened to them? What happened to their stories, their traditions, and the repository of their personal experiences? This study is an attempt to make their voices sing again, these women witnesses—and in so doing, breech the silence of the centuries, probing to the heart of the mystery that is the gospel of John.

Who was Jesus, after all? Was he the wholly divine being who came solely to die for our sins, and the sins of all humanity, whose whole life was about sacrifice for an imperfect humanity? Or was he just a small-town rabbi who taught an appealing version of humanistic behavior, a man who was made divine by the machinations of a politician? Or was he the focus of the zealots who hoped to put him on the throne of Israel, the willing (or unwilling) heir to David's kingship? This question of faith can only be answered by each individual believer. Each gospel presents an understanding of Jesus that reflects the community that produced that gospel. What this book tries to do is get inside the mind of the writer of the gospel of John, to examine the structure of the gospel in order to perceive what that writer and preacher and evangelist is telling us about the role of women in the community of faith that gave birth to this book.

In many ways the gospels of Mark, Matthew, and Luke center around the disciples, their calls, the miracles worked in their presence, and the teachings for their benefit. In these, the synoptic gospels, the disciples are forever witnessing yet not seeing the miracles of healing; hearing yet not understanding the words of grace and revelation. If we study the synoptic gospels side by side, we discover that all three share the basic structure: the "skeleton" of Mark's account, with additional material in both Luke and Matthew. The gospel of John, on the other hand, presents the saving message of Jesus in a radically different way. The major themes of this gospel are revealed through a series of seven encounters between Jesus and, not the twelve disciples, but women of diverse backgrounds and religious identity. This series of encounters forms the backbone, the structure of the gospel of John. Unlike the synoptic gospels, the gospel of John seems to have a female skeleton.

What secret lies here, in this book? In the other gospels, Mary the mother of Jesus, though necessarily present at his birth, is otherwise portrayed as a woman who worries and whom Jesus must dismiss. Martha of Bethany is a fussbudget who must be reminded that she is missing the point. Mary of Bethany is confused with a sinful woman. The important moments in the structure of the gospels, such as revealing the identity of Jesus, the message of Jesus, and the imparting of all that powerful and mysterious language about life and glory—all those moments are spent with his male disciples. There is a certain logic to that, we assume, since they were his companions, the ones to whom Jesus entrusted his ministry…weren't they? So why would the writer of the gospel of John turn the stories upside down and tell us that it was not in the baptism of Jesus that he took the first step on the road to Calvary and glory, but in the miracle of the wine at Cana, at the behest of his mother? Why, when Jesus revealed his Messiahship to Peter in the other gospels, would he reveal that glorious truth in the gospel of John to a nameless woman of ill repute encountered by chance at a well in hostile territory? And why would Jesus describe the nature of salvation, in other gospels the subject of the great sermons on mount and plain, to an angry, disappointed, and challenging Samaritan woman? Why, most powerfully and poignantly of all, did Jesus reveal his victory over death, ignoring Peter to whom he had given "the keys to the kingdom," passing by John and James, and even the disciple called "the beloved," and appear first instead to Mary Magdalene, sending her as the apostle to the apostles?

Many of us grew up with only a sketchy acquaintance with the many women whose stories march through the pages of the Old and New Testaments, women of valor and of nobility, women whose courage, sacrifice, wisdom, and love of God helped to build the stories of faith we treasure today. Their stories were not told, and their heroism was unsung. Today, however, more and more scholars are turning their attention to the stories of those women of valor, these mothers of the faith. They are everywhere in the Bible, but nowhere are they as prominent and as central as in the gospel of John. This gospel does not just include stories about women, it is structured around stories of women. In this unique testament, women and their encounters with Jesus provide the framework for the central message of Jesus. They are, in a sense, the heartbeat of John's gospel.

The structure of this book revolves around an exploration of the themes and structure of the gospel of John. This exploration involves both exegesis and homiletics. That is, each chapter begins with an exploration of the texts, referencing a variety of scholars' views and ideas about their meaning. A reflection, or sermon, follows the exegetical section. Each reflection expresses the way the material entered my life and understanding, the personal meaning and power I find there, and what I believe to be the message that applies to all who attempt to live the Jesus life. I have preached all these reflections to my congregations—either on Sundays, where they are the texts from the Revised Common Lectionary, or as part of the seminar entitled "Driving Away the Dark."

The Appendices and my Web site (www.judithkayejones.com) include additional material from my history with the gospel of John. In the Appendices I include a seven-week study guide for those who might like to use this book for a Bible study or Christian education event. Following the study guide is a seven-week worship design. This design includes music and dramatic readings that can be used in worship services focused on the women in the gospel of John. Music includes traditional and contemporary hymns, as well as original compositions. The dramatic readings are also part of *The Women's Tale,* the play that ends the Appendices. You may present this play on Easter Sunday morning, at the conclusion of the six-week study mentioned above. It is my hope that the reflections following each chapter, as well as the dramatic readings and music suggestions, may help the reader or worship team in putting together such a series.

It is my profound hope that in exploring the texts, midrash, and worship materials provided here, the readers will find the voices of the women in the gospel of John singing to them of their own profound experiences of Jesus and the way he changes and empowers lives.

1

New Wine

O n the third day there was a wedding in Cana of
Galilee, and the mother of Jesus was there. Jesus and
his disciples had also been invited to the wedding. When the
wine gave out, the mother of Jesus said to him, "They have no
wine." And Jesus said to her, "Woman, what concern is that to
you and to me? My hour has not yet come." His mother said to
the servants, "Do whatever he tells you." Now standing there
were six stone water jars for the Jewish rites of purification, each
holding twenty or thirty gallons. Jesus said to them, "Fill the
jars with water." And they filled them up to the brim. He said
to them, "Now draw some out, and take it to the chief steward."
So they took it. When the steward tasted the water that had
become wine, and did not know where it came from (though the
servants who had drawn the water knew), the steward called the
bridegroom and said to him, "Everyone serves the good wine
first, and then the inferior wine after the guests have become
drunk. But you have kept the good wine until now." Jesus did
this, the first of his signs, in Cana of Galilee, and revealed his
glory; and his disciples believed in him.

After this he went down to Capernaum with his mother, his
brothers, and his disciples; and they remained there a few days.
(Jn. 2:1–12)

Lewis Carroll instructs the white rabbit, (and us) that in telling a tale, it
is best to "begin at the beginning and go on 'till you come to the end: then
stop."[1] But in the gospel stories of the life and ministry of Jesus, what is the

beginning, exactly? "In the beginning..." means something different in all the gospels. In the beginning of Mark's gospel, we meet Jesus on the road, engaged in ministry, rushing everywhere "immediately." With breathless haste we read of the baptism of Jesus, the divine acknowledgment of his identity by a God who says, "You are my Son, the Beloved; with you I am well pleased" (1:11), and the calling of disciples to the healing, saving ministry of the Messiah. Clearly Mark is uninterested in the circumstances of Jesus' birth. There is no cold desert night, no choir of angels, no rude stable or confused shepherds, no jingling of spurs or Magi gold. Jesus' identity will be revealed to us as we are propelled along the road of his unfolding ministry. Matthew's gospel, following the genealogy establishing Jesus as the heir of Abraham and Moses, begins with the angelic visitation to Joseph, reassuring him of God's plan for the child his chaste bride-to-be inexplicably carries in her womb. In a tale of terror, Matthew sends us on a desperate journey with mother, child, and earthly stepfather Joseph, away from the swords of an insecure tyrant. As with Moses, Jesus will come out of Egypt and establish the promised land of God's kingdom. Luke's genealogy, asserting Jesus as Adam's descendent and therefore heir not just of Israel but all humankind, begins with Mary herself receiving God's messenger. Luke presents us with the portrait of the sublimely obedient virgin so beloved of painters and pageants. The words of the *Magnificat,* enfleshed and clothed in shimmering blue robe and golden halo, form the centerpiece of countless representations of Mary, the mother of Jesus.

We encounter Mary, the mother of Jesus, on another occasion in the three synoptic gospels. It is a strange and troubling portrait. Mary, alarmed at Jesus' growing notoriety and fearful for his safety, presses through the crowds that surround him to plead for him to return home. It is a totally believable picture of a loving mother whose child has taken a dangerous path and who seeks to dissuade him from following it to disaster. Believable, but inconsistent with the infinitely faithful and obedient virgin of the birth narratives of Luke and Matthew. We may ponder whether the glorious mystery of Jesus' conception and birth could has faded from her memory along with the pangs of birth. For here is no exalted mother of God, accepting her son's divine destiny with a song. Here is a woman who, far from conceding all to God's will, wants only to protect her son from the unfriendly ears and hearts that surround him. Jesus' response is to repudiate her right to do so. In what seems to be a cold dismissal, he asks, "Who is my mother, and who are my brothers?" (Mt. 12:48b), and in Luke, "My mother and my brothers are those who hear the word of God and do it" (Lk. 8:21). Mary, the mother of Jesus, the bright and tender virgin of miraculous birth, is now confused and fearful, and is dismissed as a roadblock to her son's ministry. The message of the synoptics is clear. Mary's purpose is established in Luke and Matthew as the physical bearer of the Messiah, worthy by virtue of her purity and unquestioning obedience.

In all three synoptic gospels, when she attempts to assert authority over his adult ministry, she is only an impediment.

As with the annunciation and the nativity, artists have been fascinated with the picture of Mary and Jesus at a table, surrounded by (usually) beautifully dressed guests celebrating a wedding. It should be noted here that though we refer to her as Mary, as she is named in the other gospels, in the gospel of John itself she is only referred to as the "mother of Jesus." At first glance this may suggest a similar emphasis as Luke's and Matthew's gospels, in which her role as birth mother is her only valid role in Jesus' life. In fact, John's portrait of Mary is radically different from that meek and accepting virgin, and Jesus' response to her is also radically different from that recorded in the other gospels.

The gospel of John takes "In the beginning" very seriously. For this author, the beginning is neither Bethlehem nor baptism. As with Mark, there is no birth narrative in John's gospel. No single star leads us to the manger. In the lovely poetic prologue, mirroring the prologue in chapter 1 of the book of Genesis, the Christ exists before time and space as the creative Word of God, and all the stars of the cosmos are his. The details of his earthly incarnation are unimportant. We meet him in the flesh first, still in chapter 1, at his baptism, followed the next day by his recruitment of his first disciples, including Andrew and Simon. On the third day, we meet the incarnate Word, Jesus, with disciples already in tow, present at a wedding. Or rather we learn that his *mother* is at the wedding, and Jesus and his disciples had "also been invited" (Jn. 2:1–12). This order, in which Jesus' presence is subordinate to his mother's, in a gospel in which nothing is unintentional, signifies that the mother of Jesus and her presence at this wedding is of great importance. In other words, her symbolic importance is primary in this story of Jesus' first public miracle. Matthew and Luke focus their attention on Mary at the birth of Jesus. The wedding at Cana focuses on her role in the birth of his ministry.

Mary notices that the wedding is running short on wine. That this was a serious problem should be underscored. Families saved for a lifetime to afford wedding celebrations, which lasted for days, and the family honor rested on the abundance it provided. Apparently the family of the wedding party has not noticed (unless Mary was related to them, a theory some have used to explain her concern). Related or not, Mary is obviously observant and concerned. We could debate forever about why she did what she did, what her expectations were when she pointed out the absence of wine, whose wedding it in fact was, that she was so concerned, but the main point is that Mary steps out of the frame so carefully and so rigidly constructed for her in the synoptics as the totally obedient, totally passive young woman of the infancy narratives. The mother of Jesus (now being neither meek nor timorous) simply steps up and lays her concern before him: "They have no wine" (v. 3).

Jesus' response may seem emotionally similar to his response to her concern for his safety or sanity in the synoptics, as he answers, "Woman, what concern is that to you and to me? My hour has not yet come" (v. 4). Much has been written about the way Jesus addresses his mother, "woman," not by name or title. This form of address was not disrespectful, and there is no scriptural evidence that he was annoyed or speaking sharply to her. The iconic image of "woman" rather suggests that she is not just his mother but also a symbol. Whether she represented the New Eve—whose faithfulness will help Jesus, the New Adam, remedy the failure and disobedience of the originals—is an issue debated by biblical scholars.[2] What does seem obvious is that her relationship to him as his mother is not her only role. His response, "What concern is that to you and to me?" is a translation of an idiom, and seems to suggest a question rather than repudiation—"Is this our concern?" He goes on to claim that his "hour has not yet come." Here we do not have a son struggling to keep to his chosen path without her interference, as in the synoptic gospels. Their positions regarding his ministry are reversed in this story. Clearly Mary thinks it is appropriate, that it is time for Jesus to begin his ministry by doing something about the absence of wine. She ignores her son's demur, his reluctance to intervene in the situation of empty wine jars, of revealing himself before he is ready as one in whom the power of God resides. Instead, we have *her insistence* that he commit to the path and *his temporary unwillingness* to do so. There lie at hand great stone water jars "for the Jewish rites of purification" (v. 6). Imbedded in this complex story is the realization that the old covenant, represented by the water for purification rituals, is being superseded by the new covenant, a covenant that will be celebrated and remembered and recreated with wine, symbol of Christ's blood sealing us forever in an intimate, life-giving relationship with God.

The story appears to be simplicity itself when it comes to Mary. She points out the need she has observed and she is not discouraged when he is unwilling to act. She exhibits perfect faith when, in spite of her son's demur, she turns to the servants and says, "Do whatever he tells you" (v. 5). Surely Mary's concern is not simply that there is not enough wine at a wedding celebration. The narrative is about ministry, about Jesus' commitment to being revealed as the Messiah, and his mother's faith as his first disciple.

The text tells us that, upon seeing the good wine flowing where once there was only water, "his disciples believed in him" (v. 11). They will continue to respond to miracles throughout the gospel in this way; continue to grope through the darkness toward the light of truth. But they never quite see, until after the resurrection. Mary, the mother of Jesus, already is where the disciples must yet go; she is the disciple who already believes and believes absolutely. This first miracle, revealing the astonishing love and power of God that will triumph over the past, occurs on "the third day," pointing to another third day in which that power will be revealed to triumph even over death. This woman is the mother not only of Jesus but of the ministry, and that ministry is initiated by the Messiah at her prompting. This Mary asks for—and receives new wine.

REFLECTION: New Wine

There is a lot of buzz about the Virgin Mary nowadays, even in the previously resistant halls of Protestant thought. Kathleen Norris, best-selling author of *Dakota*[3] and the *Cloister Walk*,[4] has published a book about the need for Protestants to rediscover the mother of Jesus.[5] She argues that we are missing something essential, some part of the divine revelation in our insistence that Mary be limited to a once-a-year appearance at Christmas, calling to mind the songs of angels in a cold clear sky above the desert town called Bethlehem.

As a Protestant, I grew up relatively unacquainted with Mary, the mother of Jesus. In the days before the Common Lectionary, she was rarely mentioned. Oh, we heard about her at Christmas as she approached that manger bed where she would give birth to the baby Jesus. Mary existed on the edges of my church life, occasionally mentioned in the lesson as she sought for her son in the temple, or when she tried to persuade Jesus to stop inciting the crowds to riot, and, of course, when she appeared on Christmas Eve in her blue robe surrounded by tiny ebullient angels and shy shepherds wearing bathrobes in our annual pageant. Mary was a mysterious and puzzling figure. In some of my friends' churches, she was a gilded statue standing amid offerings of flowers and prayer cards. Protestants viewed such representations with grave suspicion, and I knew that somehow devotion to Mary was "too Catholic."

I do remember one sermon about Mary, however. I had an uncle who liked to read theology, and he had told me that the virgin birth was a myth and that Joseph was the father of Jesus. This troubled me, and so I asked the minister of my church. "What about the virgin birth? Is it really true?" I remember his answer. After preaching about the literal truth of Mary's virginity, he said, "This is not just a question. It is the *only* question." His point was that we could not call ourselves Christians if we did not believe in the virgin birth.

I suppose I remembered the sermon at first, because the minister preached it especially for me. Over the years, however, that special sermon became a burden to me. I am not a biblical literalist, and as an adult I was troubled by all the emphasis on Mary's perfect obedience and her perpetual virginity. I had friends whose lives were made a burden by being reminded that they had to be obedient if they were to "be like Mary." Every task, every test, every moment of their lives was loaded with that precept. Never disagree, never argue, never refuse; be like Mary. And I became aware that sexuality was dangerous, and somehow dirty, and it was better to be pure—that is, *virgin,* like Mary. Eventually I turned my back on Mary. I could find no comfort there. I was a woman, but I would never make it on anybody's "most obedient" list. I was a woman, and I wanted a happy marriage and children, so I would certainly not be a perpetual virgin. I longed to embrace the feminist ideals of self-determinism and liberation, to feel empowered and whole, to be proud of my woman's body and awed and appreciative of its power to provide pleasure and nurture. If I wanted to live life as a strong, fulfilled woman, I could never "be like Mary."

It was in seminary that I encountered the gospel of John, and the radical, strong, Jewish mother whose faith never wavered. In the other gospels, Jesus' ministry begins with his healing of those multitudes of sick and suffering people who came to hear his teaching. But in the gospel of John, his public ministry begins not amid the suffering of ordinary days but during the joyful occasion of a wedding. He and his mother are guests. You know the story. The wine gave out. If the wedding feast had run out of wine, the entire family would have been shamed, not just for a day or two, but for the rest of their lives. And here we have Jesus' mother, the observant and concerned woman who perceives that the wine has run out. She tells her son simply, "They have no wine" (v. 3). Now Mary does not say this as an idle comment. She clearly expects Jesus to do something about it. She clearly knows he *can* do something about it. She has faith in his ability to turn tragedy into joy, to bring life to what is barren, and give fullness to what is empty. This is the central point about the mother of Jesus in this story. Mary, as we know her, is a mother who clearly believes her son can do anything he wants to do. She immediately turns to the servants and says, again with perfect faith, "Do whatever he tells you" (v. 5). Standing by are huge jars used to hold ritually pure water. Jesus, seeing perhaps in his mother's face her faith and her strength and courage, draws courage also from her, and turns to the servants and tells them to fill the jars with water, and to draw some out. It comes out in all its amazing abundance, rich streams, gallons and gallons, an unimaginable amount of wine, and not just wine but *good* wine, the best wine. So the ministry of Jesus begins at his mother's behest, resting on her faith and strength of purpose, the new wine of the gospel, the promise of abundance beyond imagination, water into wine.

I agree with Kathleen Norris that if we are to truly enter into the mystery that is God with whole hearts and open minds, we must restore a sense of the divine feminine to the overwhelmingly masculine understanding most of us grew up with.[6] I also agree that restoring Mary to her place as a salvific figure— a feminine understanding of the saving acts of God—is a good place to start. However, it must be a new Mary. For me, it cannot be the passive, meek, perpetual virgin who lives forever behind an ageless face and an immaculate blue robe. Though I will always enjoy the pageants at

Christmas, with Mary center stage, I like the Mary at Cana better because I understand her better. I trust her because she does not require of me some impossible state of perfect obedience and purity. She was a woman who lived life fully and loved deeply. Mary must be resurrected as the woman who taught Jesus when he was little, whose influence sent him out a radically inclusive man who saw women as fully human and worthy to participate in the kingdom. Where, after all, do we think he learned it? Mary must be liberated from the too sweet, permanently virgin, sexless, and basically life-denying figure she has become for too many people for too many centuries, if she is to speak to my woman's heart with her true power.

Notes

[1] Lewis Carroll, *Alice's Adventures in Wonderland.*

[2] Gerard S. Sloyan, *John,* Interpretation: A Bible Commentary for Teaching and Preaching (Atlanta: John Knox Press, 1988), 33.

[3] Kathleen Norris, *Dakota: A Spiritual Biography* (Boston: Mariner Books, 2001).

[4] Kathleen Norris, *The Cloister Walk* (New York: Trade, 1997).

[5] Kathleen Norris, "Foreword," in *Blessed One: Protestant Perspectives on Mary,* ed. Beverly R. Gaventa and Cynthia L. Rigby (Louisville: Westminster John Knox Press, 2002). This book would have been helpful to me as I forged a meandering path through monastery retreats back to membership in a Protestant church. Rediscovering Mary was no small part of that journey, but I felt very much alone with my new understanding of her, and of her place in my life of faith. The church in which I was raised had a curious attitude toward Mary, an odd mixture of hubris and bashfulness. We dragged Mary out at Christmas, along with the angels, and placed her at center stage. Then we packed her safely in the crèche box for the rest of the year.

[6] Kathleen Norris, *Amazing Grace: A Vocabulary of Faith* (New York: Riverhead Books, 1998), 116–23.

2

Living Water

But he had to go through Samaria. So he came to a Samaritan city called Sychar, near the plot of ground that Jacob had given to his son Joseph. Jacob's well was there, and Jesus, tired out by his journey, was sitting by the well. It was about noon.

A Samaritan woman came to draw water, and Jesus said to her, "Give me a drink." (His disciples had gone to the city to buy food.) The Samaritan woman said to him, "How is it that you, a Jew, ask a drink of me, a woman of Samaria?" (Jews do not share things in common with Samaritans.) Jesus answered her, "If you knew the gift of God, and who it is that is saying to you, 'Give me a drink,'' you would have asked him, and he would have given you living water." The woman said to him, "Sir, you have no bucket, and the well is deep. Where do you get that living water? Are you greater than our ancestor Jacob, who gave us the well, and with his sons and his flocks drank from it?" Jesus said to her, "Everyone who drinks of this water will be thirsty again, but those who drink of the water that I will give them will never be thirsty. The water that I will give will become in them a spring of water gushing up to eternal life." The woman said to him, "Sir, give me this water, so that I may never be thirsty or have to keep coming here to draw water."

Jesus said to her, "Go, call your husband, and come back." The woman answered him, "I have no husband." Jesus said to her, "You are right in saying, 'I have no husband'; for you have had five husbands, and the one you have now is not your husband. What you have said is true!" The woman said to him,

"Sir, I see that you are a prophet. Our ancestors worshiped on this mountain, but you say that the place where people must worship is in Jerusalem." Jesus said to her, "Woman, believe me, the hour is coming when you will worship the Father neither on this mountain nor in Jerusalem. You worship what you do not know; we worship what we know, for salvation is from the Jews. But the hour is coming, and is now here, when the true worshipers will worship the Father in spirit and truth, for the Father seeks such as these to worship him. God is spirit, and those who worship him must worship in spirit and truth." The woman said to him, "I know that Messiah is coming" (who is called Christ). "When he comes, he will proclaim all things to us." Jesus said to her, "I am he, the one who is speaking to you."

Just then his disciples came. They were astonished that he was speaking with a woman, but no one said, "What do you want?" or, "Why are you speaking with her?" Then the woman left her water jar and went back to the city. She said to the people, "Come and see a man who told me everything I have ever done! He cannot be the Messiah, can he?" They left the city and were on their way to him.

Meanwhile the disciples were urging him, "Rabbi, eat something." But he said to them, "I have food to eat that you do not know about." So the disciples said to one another, "Surely no one has brought him something to eat?" Jesus said to them, "My food is to do the will of him who sent me and to complete his work. Do you not say, 'Four months more, then comes the harvest'? But I tell you, look around you, and see how the fields are ripe for harvesting. The reaper is already receiving wages and is gathering fruit for eternal life, so that sower and reaper may rejoice together. For here the saying holds true, 'One sows and another reaps.' I sent you to reap that for which you did not labor. Others have labored, and you have entered into their labor."

Many Samaritans from that city believed in him because of the woman's testimony, "He told me everything I have ever done." So when the Samaritans came to him, they asked him to stay with them; and he stayed there two days. And many more believed because of his word. They said to the woman, "It is no longer because of what you said that we believe, for we have heard for ourselves, and we know that this is truly the Savior of the world." (Jn. 4:4–42)

The next encounter between Jesus and a woman recorded in John's gospel takes place in the hostile territory known as Samaria, and a radical tale it is. The first point is its location. The gospel text begins by telling us that Jesus *had to go* through Samaria in order to get from Judea to Galilee. But we know that Jesus didn't *have to* go through Samaria. Good Jews of the day didn't have to go there, and they went to considerable effort to avoid it. Yet the author of John's gospel makes quite a point of the inexplicable necessity in pointing out that Jesus departed again to Galilee and he had to pass through Samaria, near a city called Sychar, which was famous because it was the location of Jacob's well. Samaria serves as a symbol of enemy territory, inhabited by the despised mongrel people who intermarried with Gentiles, whose blood was polluted, who practiced a bastardized version of Judaism, on the wrong holy mountain, and whose sanctuary had been burned down a few times in the past by the "good and righteous" Jews. Samaria was a place so vile that to eat the bread of a Samaritan was the same as eating the flesh of a pig—that is, irremediably unclean. So any observant Jews went around Samaria to avoid contaminating even the sandals on their feet, though it took an extra two days to get from Judea to Galilee that way. Yet we are told that Jesus, instead of going the "right way," deliberately goes through "no Jews land" and crosses Samaria, where he is pretty sure of meeting "one of them." Some scholars believe this reflects not an actual journey of Jesus into Samaria, but the later development of the Samaritan mission.[1] Within the context of the story, however, it is important to remember that the Jews and Samaritans despised one another, and Jesus' encounter with the woman at the well is illustrative of an inclusive understanding of discipleship. His disciples leave him at Jacob's well, a profoundly important symbol of God's love in providing water in the desert, an ancestral memory of God's saving help, now in the territory of a despised enemy. They go to find food—a challenging undertaking, since everything Samaritan is to be rejected out of hand.

And so he does meet one of them—and not just a Samaritan, but a woman.

And not just a Samaritan woman, but, as the story unfolds, an immoral Samaritan woman. Any discussion of Jesus' encounter with her must include the persistence of Jesus' grace, going there to find and single out and talk to a woman who, because of race, gender, and lifestyle, was a virtual untouchable.

As Jesus waits beside the well, the woman comes to draw water. The woman is not named, and, as in all the other stories about nameless women interacting with Jesus, some have seen in this an indifference to women's identity by gospel writers. While I agree that the gospel records seem careless about women's names, there are also important stories about men who are not identified by name. When that happens, the individual in the story is generally iconic. That is, he stands for more than an individual, representing a larger group of people. In the case of the man born blind, for example, he represents all those who do not or will not see the light of truth as proclaimed by Jesus. The woman at the well, therefore, represents a group of people as well as an individual. Surely she represents the Samaritans, but that identity alone could have (and I believe, would have) been served by using a man as the main character of the story. It is the fact that she was a woman that is the real power in this story. Just as Mary at Cana is referred to by "woman," indicating that she functions as more than just his mother in this story, so the Samaritan woman functions as more than a woman met by chance out where she should not be. The narrative carefully tells us that it was "about noon" (v. 6). The time of the encounter is significant, and so we must consider the social realities of the day that had reduced this woman to her current situation. The behavior of women was circumscribed, and this included strict limits on public gathering. The women of the town who needed to draw water at a public well went in groups, and in the morning when it was cooler. There can be only one reason the Samaritan woman would be at the well in the heat of the day, alone, and that is because she was shunned by the other women in her community. Her very presence proclaims her an outcast. This woman, who is an outcast even among the outcast people of Samaria, approaches the well and Jesus asks her for a drink of water from her own gourd. In a country where he should not take anything from the hand of a Samaritan, here he is, offering to place his lips where hers have rested, an unthinkable intimacy, mingling the essence of breath and mouth even as he will mingle the thoughts of his mind with this untouchable woman.

It is no surprise that the woman can hardly believe she has heard him correctly. When she questions Jesus about requesting a drink from her, he promises her that if she should ask he would give her living water (v. 10). In the ensuing dialogue, the woman draws a comparison between the water of the well of their ancestor Jacob, and the living water he promises. As in the story of the wedding at Cana, water is used to symbolize the old ways of thinking, old beliefs, the old covenant. The woman's response is immediate: "Sir, give me this water, so that I may never be thirsty or have to keep coming here to draw water" (v. 15). What a poignant expression of this woman's feelings. What a relief never to have to drag herself back to that well alone, in the heat of the day, a shamed and lonely woman proclaimed an outcast by her community.

Jesus goes immediately to the heart of the matter: "Go, call your husband" (v. 16). Jesus was wondering, as we are, where (who) is the man responsible for you, that you are out here alone? What has broken in your life that you are out here alone? The woman replies simply, "I have no husband" (v. 17). With no sense of accusation coming through the text, Jesus replies, "You are right..., for you have had five husbands, and the one you have now is not your husband" (vv. 17–18). There follows what, to me, is one of the funniest lines in the New Testament. "Sir," she no doubt stammers, "I see that you are a prophet!" (v. 19).

Why had she been married five times? Why was she reduced to living with a man who was not her husband? I have encountered the suggestion that she just couldn't find love, couldn't find the right man so she kept moving on. Well, nonsense. Men could divorce their wives for the most trivial of reasons, but women could not divorce their husbands for any reason whatsoever. There is some evidence women could go home to their families, but they would be a drain on the families' economic well-being, and they couldn't marry again unless their husbands divorced them or died. So was she a woman who was so hard to live with that five men had married and divorced her? It seems peculiar that the men of her community wouldn't have learned by former example. Or was she a widow five times?—well, I think that circumstance would have been noteworthy enough to make it into the story and her neighbors would have shunned her for an entirely different reason than the one given. Now she is living openly with a man who is not her husband. Fornication was, like adultery, a serious crime, so it is surprising she hadn't been stoned to death.

Here they are, at an ancient desert well tied to the deepest roots of Jewish and Samaritan heritage and identity, Jesus and this untouchable female, and they fall into a theological discussion about the coming of the Messiah. We know that the woman is witty enough to hold up her end of the conversation, and to draw important conclusions. The synoptic gospels, particularly Mark, promote a mystery scholars refer to as the "Messianic secret." Recall in the first half of Mark, Jesus' ministry of healing is often punctuated by his admonishment of the recipients of miracles to "go—but tell no one." When he does speak in self-revelatory terms, as in the gospels of Matthew and Luke, he does so in ambiguous terms: "Then he began to say to them, 'Today this scripture has been fulfilled in your hearing'" (Lk. 4:21), and, "As they were coming down the mountain, Jesus ordered them, "Tell no one about the vision until after the Son of Man has been raised from the dead" (Mt. 17:9). In the synoptic gospels, Jesus' identity is a secret to be revealed first to the inner circle of the disciples, only through references open to interpretation, to question, to misunderstanding. Here in John's gospel, he casually gives away this secret knowledge, just openly tells this unworthy woman, "I am he" (v. 26). He shares with her his deepest and most profound truth—his identity as the promised one, the Messiah of God.

The most radical point in this story, however, is not the unnecessary journey to a hated land, nor is it the willingness of Jesus to engage a socially and religiously unacceptable female in a deep theological conversation, nor is it even that he reveals himself to her as the Messiah. It is the transformation of the woman herself, who steps out of all this miasma of guilt and shame and limitation and oppression—steps out of it and goes to bring the good news to her people. Something in that exchange with Jesus has empowered her and given her voice.

The woman at the well is many things: she is a tragic figure, she is a woman of ill repute, she is capable of holding her own in an astonishing conversation with someone who shouldn't be caught dead talking to her—but most important of all, she is an evangelist. She is a preacher. She hears the truth she receives, there beside that hundred foot deep well, symbol of the past, and receives living water, moving, flowing, changing water and she is filled, and she is changed. We see her dropping the bucket, forgetting about her water jar, casting off the past in which she has no voice, ignoring the male disciples who have come up and are registering disapproval for Jesus' wasting time talking to her—she just steps out of all that and runs back to her village because she is so full of that living water she just has to go and share it. She just has to tell her people—those same people who don't talk to her, don't listen to her, probably pretend they don't even see her. Those people who have hurt her so badly for so long, condemned her to a life of loneliness and shame—it is to those people she goes, bursting with the good news, awash in living water, a veritable fountain of it.

She is empowered. She goes and tells them, and they believe in Jesus initially because of the woman's testimony. A woman could not give testimony and be believed, unless at least one man could verify her testimony. No woman could defend herself at court, or identify an assailant or be a witness for someone's guilt or innocence—no woman, by herself, had a voice. Only a man who would support her statement could give her voice. Yet this woman, this shunned and despised woman, this woman is believed! She is believed because of the empowering love and acceptance of Jesus, who saw her not as a figure to be despised, hated, and avoided; not even as a figure to be pitied and forgiven; but as a person to be empowered! I find it most affirming that the male disciples must still marvel and wonder and question and struggle to understand, argue and miss the point for another seventeen chapters, but the Samaritan woman hears, understands, accepts, goes, preaches, and converts—just on one long drink of the living water that is Jesus. There are many images of women in ministry emerging out of the long silence. But I think, now and forever, the image that speaks above all the others is that lonely woman who became a fountain, full and free. She is that one woman who was summoned to a whole new reality and did not back away, did not hang back, and did not allow her own silence to continue. She is that one woman who heard the call and answered as swiftly as a free-flowing stream: the woman at the well.

REFLECTION: Desert Darkness, Desert Light

Well, here we are, back at the well. I know it must seem like we go to this well, this well in Samaria, for our meeting with the woman we find there, year after year. Certainly she is a favorite character of mine, and we have explored her character and her transformation before. I had decided I would bypass this text this year, and I thought I was going to do it—right up until I wrote this sermon. A sermon, like life, happens while you are making other plans.

Here in the midst of this story, in addition to the well and the woman, there is that noonday sun burning down. Even as we read this story, we should probably read it on a hot summer day, outside, at noon, with the sun directly overhead, beating down and making us squint our eyes against its glory and its power. That sun soaking through this passage just wouldn't let me bypass it.

Even though she is such a familiar character to many of us, I think the story of the woman of Samaria bears at least a brief recap—just hitting the high points, as it were. Jesus is traveling from Judea to his home in Nazareth, and instead of doing what any good, observant Jew would do by bypassing the hated territory of Samaria, where the very dirt underfoot made you ritually unclean, he has chosen to walk smack through "forbidden territory." His disciples having gone off to find food, Jesus waits beside the well. Then, in the hottest part of the day, the woman comes to draw water. Jesus asks her for a drink, and in the ensuing dialogue Jesus shares with her that he possesses living water, and that he is the longed-for messiah. We know that the woman is witty enough to hold up her end of the conversation, and to draw important conclusions. She is able, in fact, to *see* through the darkness of her own personal story of deprivation and loneliness, to *see* through the structures of her day that define her in a certain way, limit her in a certain way, to *see* past the traditions of the past to a new understanding of the kingdom of God, and to *see* herself in relationship to that kingdom. Out of a dark past, a dark present, the woman sees the dawn of a new future, and of a new identity in that future. In the midst of darkness, she sees.

John loves to talk about light and darkness. His gospel is, in many ways, about blindness; most of the stories of encounters between Jesus and other people involve seeing or not seeing what God reveals. This woman sees! She leaves her water jar behind—the symbol of the past, the water of the past, the deprivations in the desert of her soul and in her life—in the past, and runs to her people, crying out, "Come and see!" And they come. And, we are told, they also believe—first the passionate conviction of her message, then the evidence of their own spiritual vision when they hear and behold Jesus—they see.

We live in a reality made up of opposites. Opposites are necessary, given the way we apprehend reality. If there were no silence, there would be no concept or understanding of sound—speech, song, or prayer. If there were no pain, we would simply not be able to understand the blessing of being without pain. And if there were no darkness, then light would not have meaning to us. So, even as the woman sees, and her people see, there must be someone who does not see, someone who can't yet see through the darkness. There must be blindness to stand against the vision in order to highlight its power.

Enter the disciples—the followers who follow in faith, and yet lack faith; who listen with attention, and yet fail to understand; who walk together in the light of day with the light of the world, yet walk in darkness and are blind. They see Jesus with the woman, and are astonished that he is speaking with her. They know enough about Jesus not to question why he is speaking with her. (Clearly they have had all the assault upon their limited vision they can deal with just by coming to this benighted place called Samaria.) But they do try to shift his attention away from her. They urge him to take thought for his own personal comfort: "Rabbi, eat something" (v. 31). Jesus, no doubt full of joy over his conversation with the woman who sees him, really sees him, tries to explain to them (yet again, and again) that he is partaking fully of what really nourishes him—sharing the good news with receptive listeners, watching the dawn break over shadowed faces, seeing the new light shining in eyes that were dark with despair or hopelessness or cynicism, feasting on new souls filled with the hovering Spirit. Jesus is speaking profoundly when he says, "I have food to eat that you do not know about" (v. 32). He then tries to show them the food that lies waiting, the fields ready for the harvest, tries to instill in them a sense of ownership of the vision. It is a harvest that has already begun with the woman at the well and her powerful witness to her people.

Everything in this remarkable gospel exists at multiple levels. Yes, it is noon, and yes, that adds to the pathos and power of the story of the woman, out in the hottest part of the day alone. But it is also the brightest time of day—the bright, overpowering light of a desert at noon. Have you ever walked in the desert at noon? The light shimmers on the ground and in the sky and puts a shining halo around everything that exists beneath the sky. The sky is itself a brilliant mantle of light, and it exists as an almost solid thing that weights down your eyes and makes them water, makes you want to squint against its power, makes you understand that light can, indeed, be unbearable, be blinding. There are no shadows cast by a noonday sun, where at other hours the shadows cast by desert suns are deep and black, deeper and blacker than any other shadows, so deep and black your eyes can't adjust quickly enough, and to come out of a desert sun into a shaded place means to be wholly and completely blind for a few moments while your eyes adjust. But at noon, when the sun is directly above us, then there are no shadows, only light, light everywhere, equally illuminating, overpowering light. How like the noonday sun is the presence, the actual physical presence of Jesus. How his light must have challenged their ability to see, must have caused their spiritual irises to close in protest against the onslaught of that light. We know that, at this moment in time, there under the hot powerful sun of desert Samaria, they still do not see. They have not yet embraced the vision. And how sad, and how prophetic, that one may believe that one walks with Jesus, and yet still walk in darkness. Yet there is one who does see, and seeing, leads others to embrace the light. The woman, nameless yet immortal in her story, is a beacon in the darkness to all who are without voice, without comfort or direction, without hope. Even more significant than her ability to understand Jesus, to really see him, is her instinctive understanding that to truly see Jesus, to truly walk in the light, is to share it with community. She cannot wait to get back to her dusty, judgmental little village and bring them, too, into the light.

Lent is a challenging time of year. It is the time of year when the winter is slowly, grudgingly giving way to spring. It is the time of "not yet." In many ways, here in California it is even more confusing than it is in parts of the world where it is green in summer, brown and sere in winter, and spring tiptoes in around about April with buds and new growth. Here, of course, we start the budding out in December with camellias, the green on the hills really gets its full splendor in January and February—well, it can't make up its mind whether to be winter or spring—so has a go at each. The sun makes an occasional appearance, but still there are dark, gloomy days and drizzle, and, of course, mud. So Lent is when spring is coming but not fully arrived, darkness is leaving but not yet gone, when light is gathering and strengthening but not blazing in full glory yet. It is the time of year when we look at the tattered remains of winter, our spiritual winters that each of us must live through and see decently interred so that the new birth that comes with spring can occur. Of course, we must walk through the gathering darkness toward Good Friday, the day when it was dark at noon—and a deeper dark than you or I shall ever know. We do that because we have to if we are to come out of the darkness and into that bright, bright sunrise. However well we try to conjure the image of Lenten darkness, with its veiled lights and subdued colors, our efforts can only represent a dim suggestion of the consuming darkness of Good Friday. We can enter, through prayer and meditation, into an acquaintance with the darkness that must have been as thick and deep and overpowering to those first disciples as was the light it seemed to have swallowed. But for you and me, we know that the light lies at the end of the journey; we know that the dawn will come after the day of darkness. As people of faith, even more importantly, we know that the light of God walks with us all through the darkness. We, too, can go to the well in the brightest part of day and not be blinded but be filled with living water, and the light that has come into the world.

Notes

[1]Sandra M. Schneiders, *Written That You May Believe: Encountering Jesus in the Fourth Gospel* (New York: Crossroad, 1999), 134–35. "The story in John 4, then, probably represents a reading back into the public ministry of Jesus the Johannine community's postresurrection experience of the Samaritan mission and the influence of the Samaritan converts within the community of the Fourth Gospel."

3

New Law

Early in the morning he came again to the temple. All
the people came to him and he sat down and began to
teach them. The scribes and the Pharisees brought a woman
who had been caught in adultery; and making her stand before
all of them, they said to him, "Teacher, this woman was caught
in the very act of committing adultery. Now in the law Moses
commanded us to stone such women. Now what do you say?"
They said this to test him, so that they might have some charge
to bring against him. Jesus bent down and wrote with his
finger on the ground. When they kept on questioning him, he
straightened up and said to them, "Let anyone among you who
is without sin be the first to throw a stone at her." And once
again he bent down and wrote on the ground. When they heard
it, they went away, one by one, beginning with the elders; and
Jesus was left alone with the woman standing before him. Jesus
straightened up and said to her, "Woman, where are they? Has
no one condemned you?" She said, "No one, sir." And Jesus
said, "Neither do I condemn you. Go your way, and from now
on do not sin again."
(Jn. 8:2–11)

The story of the adulterous woman is an orphan tale. I call it that
because most scholars believe that it does not really belong in the gospel of
John. The earliest copies of that gospel do not contain it, and the language
style and vocabulary do not match the rest of John's texts. Some scholars
believe it may be from the gospel of John, but from a different place in

the book; others find it more synchronous with the gospel of Luke. Most scholars, however, think it comes from somewhere else entirely–an orphan text, adopted into the gospel of John. For a time, it was actually printed at the bottom of the page in the RSV, as a footnote. I remember feeling outrage and a sense of loss when I discovered that, because this story speaks to my heart in a particular way. Now, however, it has been restored to the body of the text, accompanied by an explanatory note that it does not appear in the earliest manuscripts. There is something about the story, however, that compelled its inclusion. The voice of Jesus, his message of compassion and forgiveness, rings so true in the story of the adulterous woman, it is considered "scriptural," representing a genuine event in the ministry of Jesus, and so is allowed to live in the place it has occupied for so many centuries, a story of amazing grace.

The narrative itself presents what appears to be a simple story of judgment. Jesus is in the temple, teaching to the crowds that have gathered around him. The Jews and Pharisees bring a woman, caught in the very act of adultery. They say to Jesus, "Now in the law Moses commanded us to stone such women. Now what do you say?" The gospel writer tells us that they did this to trap Jesus into either passing judgment under the law of Moses, knowing that the Roman occupation denied the Jews the power to carry out capital punishment, or denying the law of Moses, and setting the people against him. Jesus declines to be trapped between secular and religious law. Either of these answers would deny the truth Jesus has been teaching, laid out in the previous seven chapters of the gospel. He neither affirms the Mosaic tradition by saying, "Fulfill the law–stone her," nor does he deny it and say, "Set her free." Bending down, Jesus writes something in the dirt on the floor of the temple. What he wrote there is not told to us, although it is subject for much conjecture for exegetes and sermon writers. (Some later manuscripts tell of Jesus writing "the sins of each of them." Others suggest it was the Seventh Commandment. Still others that it was mere doodling, to distract the accusers and distance Jesus from those gathered around him. Finally, Jesus looks up and says, "Let anyone among you who is without sin be the first to throw a stone at her." He then continues writing his mysterious message in the dirt. No one being willing to claim sinlessness, one by one those gathered there slip away, beginning with the elders. It is only when Jesus and the woman are left alone that he speaks to her at all. "Woman, where are they? Has no one condemned you?" (v. 10). She replies, "No one, sir." And Jesus says, "Neither do I condemn you. Go your way, and from now on do not sin again" (v. 11).

Though the story is simple, it is not without its mysteries. Who was this unnamed woman? What was the message written in the dirt by Jesus? The very oddness of this detail, something not identified written in the dirt of the temple floor, teases our imaginations. It is not, after all, essential to the story. Jesus could have simply replied to the demand for judgment in the same way without writing in the dust. It does not serve to divert the accusers from their purpose, for the text tells us that, while he was writing, "they kept on questioning him" (v. 7). Then there is the mystery of the story's inclusion in the gospel of John in this particular place. It apparently was not original to the gospel of John, but was added later. The authenticity of its message, however, has kept it part of the text, though it has moved at various times from margins to footnote and back to the body of the text. If it was added later, or moved from some other place in the book as some suggest, is it's current location important or not?

With regard to the woman's identity, we can only deduce who she is not. Some ancient traditions identified her, along with the also unnamed sinful woman in Luke who washed Jesus' feet with her tears, as Mary Magdalene. There is no scriptural evidence that Mary Magdalene was a sinner, except in that she was a human being, as are we all. When the writer of the gospel of John does refer to Mary Magdalene later in the text, he does so by name, so clearly it was known to him. It seems likely that this coupling of Mary Magdalene with the woman taken in adultery (and also with the woman of Samaria who scandalously had five husbands plus one) served to shift the focus away from Mary Magdalene as witness, teacher, and apostle.[1] As with the woman at the well, the adulterous woman must remain nameless, for her importance is not as a specific individual, but as a symbol of victimization by hypocrisy, unjust law, and the failure of compassion.

In answer to the last question, the placement of this story of judgment and grace lies imbedded in surrounding texts about judgment. The gospel of John is filled with references to Mosaic law, and to the traditions of the prophets. The gospel writer first establishes the heart of this theme at the end of the prologue, where he writes: "The law was given through Moses; grace and truth came through Jesus Christ" (1:17). He develops this theme with references to the prophets, the frequent coupling of the names of Moses and Jesus, and by comparing and contrasting their authority and power.

John establishes Jesus as the messianic hope of prophecy: "Philip found Nathaniel and said to him, 'We have found him about whom Moses in the law and also the prophets wrote, Jesus son of Joseph from Nazareth'" (1:45).

He compares Moses, who was God's instrument of salvation in the wilderness, with Jesus, whose lifting up on a cross will bring ultimate salvation to those who believe: "And just as Moses lifted up the serpent in the wilderness, so must the Son of man be lifted up, that whoever believes in him may have eternal life" (3:14).

He asserts that Jesus' authority to judge comes directly from God, who has given judgment over to the Son:

"The Father judges no one but has given all judgment to the Son." (5:22)

"For just as the Father has life in himself, so he has granted the Son also to have life in himself; and he has given him authority to execute judgment, because he is the Son of Man." (5:26–27)

"I can do nothing on my own. As I hear, I judge; and my judgment is just, because I seek not my own will but the will of him who sent me." (5:30)

He points out the failure of Israel to find salvation in the Law:

"Do not think that I shall accuse you before the Father; your accuser is Moses, on whom you set your hope. If you believed Moses, you would believe me, for he wrote about me." (5:45–46)

"Did not Moses give you the law? Yet none of you keeps the law." (7:19a)

Having incurred the condemnation of the Pharisees for healing the paralyzed man on the Sabbath (when no work or unnecessary action was to be undertaken), he points out the dichotomy of obeying the law by breaking it: "If a man receives circumcision on the sabbath in order that the law of Moses may not be broken, are you angry with me because on the Sabbath I healed a man's whole body on the sabbath?" (7:23).

Perhaps most pertinent, he concludes his rebuttal with this pronouncement about judgment: "Do not judge by appearances, but judge with right judgment" (7:24).

Chapter 8 begins with the story of the woman taken in adultery. This attempt to trap Jesus by forcing him to sit in judgment on her points to the failure of judgment under Mosaic law to lead the people to righteousness. The woman, who has apparently been taken in the very act of adultery, is alone in her shame. The law specified that both the man and the woman should be brought to judgment. It is, after all, impossible to commit adultery by oneself. Yet the man who shares her guilt does not share in her trial. No witnesses are recorded as being present. Neither the motives of her accusers nor the evidence presented constitute an appropriate trial under the law of Moses, whose name and authority they invoke.

Following this story, Jesus continues his conversation with those gathered in the temple who have, presumably, returned once the mock trial was over. He continues to reiterate the difference between the way justice has been perverted under the law and the way his divine Father would have it be: "You judge by human standards; I judge no one. Yet even if I do judge, my judgment is valid; for it is not I alone who judge, but I and the Father who sent me. In your law it is written that the testimony of two witnesses is valid. I testify on my own behalf, and the Father who sent me testifies on my behalf" (8:15–18).

Following as it does the story of the woman taken in adultery, we see that the story serves as the concrete example of the two approaches to justice and judgment. The woman has been dragged to the temple and placed before him as one "caught in the very act of committing adultery" (v. 4). Three or four key people necessary to a just trial are missing. The two witness required by the law to make such an accusation do not step up and testify. Neither is the man who was equally guilty in committing this sin present or accused. Her husband, whether one of the witnesses or not, is not mentioned as being present, demanding that she be subjected to judgment.

The mysterious writing on the ground may hold the key. Numbers 5:16–31 gives the law regarding a woman believed to have committed adultery, but with no witnesses to her sin.[2] There is a trial by ordeal described in which the accused woman is taken to the temple, shamed by having her hair uncovered in public, and forced to stand before the Lord. The priest mixes holy water with "some of the dust that is on the floor of the tabernacle" (v. 16). Then the priest writes a series of curses on parchment, then washes the ink off into the water of bitterness. The woman must drink this concoction, and should the curses come true and she suffer "bitter pain" (v. 27) and illness, she is deemed guilty and shall become "an execration among her people." Should these symptoms not come upon her, then she is innocent. Four details of this extraordinary ritual are striking. The woman is taken to the temple by her husband and publicly humiliated. Dirt from the temple floor is mixed in the water. The accusation and accompanying curses are written down and the words symbolically washed off into the brew she is to drink. This ritual is specifically for the trial of a woman whose husband believes her to have committed adultery, but against whom there are no witnesses. The common elements of this story of trial by ordeal under the law and the story of the adulterous woman are evocative: temple, dirt, writing, witnesses. There in the temple, the very place prescribed for the trial by ordeal for a woman accused of adultery, Jesus leans down and writes something in the dirt of the temple floor. None of the learned scribes or Pharisees could have failed to catch the reference to the ordeal. Under the law this ordeal is only for women against whom there are no witnesses, and her husband must be present. In the case of the woman presumably taken in adultery, there do not seem to be any witnesses; nor is her husband mentioned. There must be either witnesses to the act of adultery, or a husband whose jealousy accuses her without proof. Neither is present on this occasion. The law has not been upheld by any of the accusers.

Of course, the text tells us that the scribes and Pharisees are far more interested in trapping Jesus into a false step than in justice for the sin of adultery. Is the woman even guilty of adultery, or is she just a helpless victim to be used against Jesus? This is another mystery upon which we can only speculate. The woman remains an example, whether guilty of adultery or not, as a victim of law unjustly applied. The judgment sought by the scribes and Pharisees points to their willingness to pervert the law for their own ends. And the placement of this iconic story of judgment, between Jesus' assertion that the law of Moses and those entrusted with the law have failed, and that he, and through him the Father, judge with right judgment is perfect.

Just as we were given the new wine of Christ's love and sacrifice at Cana, and were given the new living water of the Holy Spirit in Christ at the Samaritan well, so here we are given the new law of compassion and forgiveness.

REFLECTION: The Sound of Stones Falling

Pick up your rock. There we are, in the heat of the day, righteous church-going folk, leaders of the religious community well to the fore, with two agendas in our hearts: (1) We want to minimize, if possible remove, a threat to our religious security and understanding, a threat that troubles our thoughts and dreams, a threat that makes us feel that—well, perhaps what we have always believed isn't exactly right, isn't exactly enough. We just can't face the thought of having to change those old, dear, familiar beliefs that have served us for so long. Jesus, this man Jesus—well, he just has to go, that's all, and here's the way to do it. We'll put him in the position of having to make a decision, one with no good outcome or answer, along the lines of, "When did you stop beating your wife?" See, there is no way to answer that question without incriminating yourself. Our other agenda, always there in the background at least, is (2) the need to remind people of what the law is, and what their place is, and that they'd better keep it or else. All these disturbing new ideas about women following along with this itinerant preacher, daring to be out in the middle of the day, daring to talk to people as if they were men, daring to be different, and flouting the rules need to stop. Our society rests upon certain norms, certain understanding of the status quo, so it's time to let them know just what comes to women who step outside what society and the law have prescribed for them. We'll take this woman, caught in the act of adultery, and ask Jesus—oh, most respectfully, most pleasantly and even reverently—how he interprets the law regarding her as given by our most famous, central religious figure, Moses. If he says let her go (he has this most disturbing, upsetting way of looking at things—healing the sick who deserve to suffer because they are, after all, sinners or they wouldn't be sick, you know), well, if he says let her go, he is flouting the law of Moses and so he will lose all credibility with the people. And if he says "sure, right, stone her," well, we all know the Romans reserve the right to execute people for themselves, though to be sure they look the other way over these cases of adulterous women, but if anyone gets in trouble over killing this worthless sinner it will be he who pronounced judgment. Either way, we'll have made an example of her to all presumptuous women who step outside the law. So we get this sinner, and we get Jesus—you might say, two birds with one stone. So, go on, pick up your stone and hold it in your hand, get ready because the fun—er, I mean, the righteous, pious act of cleansing and retribution—is about to begin.

And then, this man Jesus, confronted by our pious leaders, seeing us righteously demanding retribution, that this sinner among us pay with her life, smelling blood, reveling in her terror and humiliation, the prospect of spectacle, seeing all that, he disassociated himself from us all, as if he couldn't bear to look us in the face. We kept asking him—what are you writing, what are you doing, but he just wouldn't respond, he kept looking away, looking down, he and the woman, both with their eyes on the ground. He kept on writing something in the dirt, the way the Roman consuls write out their judgments before they pronounce them. Then he did finally look at us, standing there with the rocks in our hands—you've still got your rock, haven't you? He looked at us and, somehow, those rocks got heavier and heavier, unbearably heavy in our hands. He looked at us and then he said, "He among you who is without sin, throw the first stone at her." The silence grew like a cloud—thick, sour, hot silence. Then there was this sound, this strange, sad little sound of admission and shame. One after another, thump, thump, into the dust, the sound of stones falling as we turned and walked away.

Come back, dear friends, to the twenty-first century. What a relief, to be here in the safe, sane present. Oh—you think you can put your rock down now, do you? Not yet, not quite yet. Like an eerie echo from the past, there was the case of a woman named Amina Lawal who lives in Nigeria. She was married for the first time when she was—well, she doesn't actually know how old she was, but it was before her first period. She was divorced and married again, and then divorced again. Her husbands just said, three times, "I divorce you," and it was over. She had no status, no protector, no hope until the next husband took her in. There need be no grounds for divorce, you understand? A husband just says the magic words and you are out. So Amina was divorced for the third time, and a little over nine months later she gave birth to a daughter. The people of her village demanded she be stoned to death for adultery. Amina insisted that the father of her child promised her marriage, but he abandoned her and later denied being the baby's father. Three male witnesses testified on his behalf that he had not had sexual relations with Amina Lawal. (Do we want to know how they knew this?) Under Shariah law, three male witnesses constitute adequate corroboration of his innocence, and he was freed. Amina was tried and convicted by her Muslim state's court, and in March 2002 she was convicted of adultery and sentenced to death. Under the strict Shariah law, pregnancy outside marriage is sufficient evidence for a woman to be convicted. She was to be taken out and buried up to the neck, when the villagers were to hit her with fist-sized stones until her head was crushed, or torn completely off, until she bled to death, her lungs collapsed, and she died. But her execution was put off until she could wean her baby daughter. Her case was appealed to Nigeria's Supreme Court, and a worldwide protest and letter-writing campaign led by Amnesty International and other world human rights organizations arose, until finally over a million letters were sent to the President of Nigeria demanding that this hideous execution be stopped. Finally, after several postponements, the case was thrown out of court, due to irregularity in the original hearings. The Constitution of Nigeria forbids execution by stoning, and repudiates the whole Muslim legal system as it is practiced in a few of its states. However, it upholds the rights of the states, as indeed we in the United States do. Therefore, the government of Nigeria is between a rock and a hard place when it intervenes in the court decisions of its member states. Notice, it did not overturn the conviction based on cruel and inhuman punishment, or on any question of the woman's right to be self-determining in her human relationships, but on legal process alone. Amina is free, and her lawyer Hauwa Ibrahim, said: "This a great victory for justice. The law of justice has prevailed over the law of man. Amina is free to go, to do what she wants."[3] Not everyone was pleased, of course. One man who attended the hearing said, "I would have preferred Amina to be stoned to death. She deserves it."[4]

Three other persons in Nigeria are currently under sentence of death by stoning: a man and a woman who are accused together of adultery, and a man accused of homosexual relationships.

Are you about to take a deep breath of relief, thinking that we don't live somewhere like that? Well, don't get comfortable. The United States, which is one of the last Western nations that still imposes the death penalty, executed fifty-nine people during 2004, with the fourth highest number of executions in the world. Many of those people had committed horrible crimes, showing no mercy themselves, and so, had little reason to expect any. However, as Gandalf, the wizard in J. R. R. Tolkien's *The Lord of the Rings,* advises Frodo, "Many that live deserve death. And some that die deserve life. Can you give it to them? Then be not too eager to deal out death in the name of justice, fearing for your own safety. Even the wise cannot see all ends."[5] It is not a question of what crimes should command the death penalty, nor how old someone must be to be given the death penalty, nor is it about the means of execution. In the end, we come down to this. We do not create the divine spark of life, and it is not ours to destroy no matter what the crime. This issue has been controversial since I was in high school, and continues to be passionately argued. But currently we are the last of the Western nations that still executes people. We have to hold onto those stones a bit longer, it seems.

Jesus looked at the woman taken in adultery, in the very act of adultery, and told her he did not condemn her. He forgave her. He modeled God's forgiveness. Many people who read this story find its significance to be the amazing, impossible forgiveness of God. This woman has, whether alone or combined with Mary Magdalene, represented that ultimate forgiveness of God. If God could forgive her, the reasoning goes, then God can surely forgive you and me. Yet we cannot somehow internalize the message. In my opinion, if all the people in mental institutions could actually accept the idea of God's forgiveness, actually believe they were forgiven, there would be a mass exodus from those places of torment and misery. Yet we cling to our guilt and sin, allowing it to alienate us from God. And that alienates us from one another.

This woman, orphaned in the gospel of John for all these centuries, cut off from her whole story, her whole context, has stood for sin for all the centuries, and the words of Jesus, "Everyone who looks at a woman with lust has already committed adultery in his heart" (Mt. 5:27), have just been glossed over. It's so easy to pin sin and guilt to that lone, orphaned woman. Side by side with our inability to accept forgiveness from God is our inability to forgive one another. Why do we have such an easy time identifying what Jesus would/did do, and such an impossible time regulating our lives by doing the same? It is easy to distance ourselves from the "too divine" Jesus. We don't have to be as forgiving as he was, because he was divine and we are not. Yet that is the heart of the story–the bedrock, as it were. All we have to do to truly experience what is already ours, the forgiveness of God, is to forgive one another–to build our society not on retribution but on compassion and understanding and, yes, forgiveness. Imagine such a world, a world where the love of God is mirrored by the love we hold for one another. Listen–what is that sound? Oh, yes–it must be the sound of stones...falling.

Notes

[1]Karen L. King, *The Gospel of Mary of Magdala: Jesus and the First Woman Apostle* (Santa Rosa, Calif.: Polebridge Press) 151–52.

[2]For a fuller treatment of this passage, see Ellen Frankel, *The Five Books of Miriam: A Woman's Commentary on the Torah* (San Francisco, Calif.: HarperSanFrancisco), 200–202.

[3]Posted on CNN.com by Jeff Koinange, "Woman Sentenced to Death Freed," Feb. 23, 2004.

[4]Ibid.

[5]J. R. R. Tolkien, *The Fellowship of the Ring,* Part 1 of *The Lord of the Rings* (Boston: Houghton Mifflin, 1999 [1954]), 68–69.

4

New Hope

Now a certain man was ill, Lazarus of Bethany, the village of Mary and her sister Martha. Mary was the one who anointed the Lord with perfume and wiped his feet with her hair; her brother Lazarus was ill. So the sisters sent a message to Jesus, "Lord, he whom you love is ill." But when Jesus heard it, he said, "This illness does not lead to death; rather it is for God's glory, so that the Son of God may be glorified through it." Accordingly, though Jesus loved Martha and her sister and Lazarus, after having heard that Lazarus was ill, he stayed two days longer in the place where he was.

Then after this he said to the disciples, "Let us go to Judea again." The disciples said to him, "Rabbi, the Jews were just now trying to stone you, and are you going there again?" Jesus answered, "Are there not twelve hours of daylight? Those who walk during the day do not stumble, because they see the light of this world. But those who walk at night stumble, because the light is not in them." After saying this, he told them, "Our friend Lazarus has fallen asleep, but I am going there to awaken him." The disciples said to him, "Lord, if he has fallen asleep, he will be all right." Jesus, however, had been speaking about his death, but they thought that he was referring merely to sleep. Then Jesus told them plainly, "Lazarus is dead. For your sake I am glad I was not there, so that you may believe. But let us go to him." Thomas, who was called the Twin, said to his fellow disciples, "Let us also go, that we may die with him."

When Jesus arrived, he found that Lazarus had already been in the tomb four days. Now Bethany was near Jerusalem, some

two miles away, and many of the Jews had come to Martha
and Mary to console them about their brother. When Martha
heard that Jesus was coming, she went and met him, while Mary
stayed at home. Martha said to Jesus, "Lord, if you had been
here, my brother would not have died. But even now I know
that God will give you whatever you ask of him." Jesus said
to her, "Your brother will rise again." Martha said to him, "I
know that he will rise again in the resurrection on the last day."
Jesus said to her, "I am the resurrection and the life. Those who
believe in me, even though they die, will live, and everyone
who lives and believes in me will never die. Do you believe
this?" She said to him, "Yes, Lord, I believe that you are the
Messiah, the Son of God, the one coming into the world."
(Jn. 11:1–27)

Before we can begin on the gospel of John's portrayal of Martha
of Bethany, we need to look at Luke and the story we find there of two
sisters. Their characters are so well established in the Lukan story, it sheds
considerable light on the role the sisters play in the gospel of John. As in
almost all gospel stories, location of the text is very important. In Luke's
gospel, the story in which we first meet Martha of Bethany and her sister
Mary follows the "lawyer's question" and the tale of the good Samaritan
(Lk. 10:25–37). The lawyer asks, "What must I do to inherit eternal life?"
(10:25b). Jesus elicits from him a declaration of not just the law, but also
how the lawyer understands it. The lawyer answers, "You shall love the
Lord your God with all your heart, and with all your soul, and with all your
strength, and with all your mind; and your neighbor as yourself" (10:27).
Jesus elicits testimony that there is one rule, not two, that to love God is to
love neighbor, and vice versa. Not two commandments, but just one, a single
coin with two faces. And then Luke continues, with Jesus saying, "Do this,
and you will live." Jesus follows this encounter with two stories, describing
how to love God, and how to love your neighbor. To describe the way to
love your neighbor, he tells the story that is a model for Christian love and
neighborliness–that is, the story of the good Samaritan. It is the classic story
about what love means, not only about what it means to be a neighbor, but
also what it means to love your neighbor. Then, Jesus goes on to tell us how
it is to love God, in this humble little tale of Martha and Mary:

Now as they went on their way, he entered a certain village, where
a woman named Martha welcomed him into her home. She had a
sister named Mary, who sat at the Lord's feet and listened to what
he was saying. But Martha was distracted by her many tasks; so
she came to him and asked, "Lord, do you not care that my sister
has left me to do all the work by myself? Tell her then to help me."
But the Lord answered her, "Martha, Martha, you are worried and

distracted by many things; there is need of only one thing. Mary has chosen the better part, which will not be taken away from her." (Lk. 10:38-32)

Bethany is not mentioned by name here, only a "certain village." There is no mention of Lazarus, the brother, who plays a crucial role in the gospel of John. Luke describes the home as belonging to Martha. She receives Jesus into her house, and we are told her sister Mary "sat at the Lord's feet and listened to what he was saying" (v. 39). Worn out with trying to take care of her guests, Martha complains. It is immediately clear that both sisters have a unique relationship with Jesus. Women in Jesus' time did not sit with the men nor were they allowed to engage a rabbi in conversation. Rabbi Eliezer wrote in the first century C.E.: "Rather should the words of the Torah be burned than entrusted to a woman...Whoever teaches his daughter the Torah is like one who teaches her obscenity."[1] Yet Mary sits at Jesus' feet, in with the men who have gathered to listen. Martha, feeling abused to be left to do all the serving work, feels free to bustle in and command Jesus to remedy her wrong. She expresses no shame or worry about Mary being in her unconventional and even scandalous place, but rather demands what she sees as justice, and she does so in a familiar and intimate way. There is no suggestion in the little exchange of shyness or the formality due a guest. Martha demands that the Lord pay attention to the situation, and make Mary abandon her place and go back to work.

Jesus speaks very gently to Martha, and explains that all the busyness is not as important as sitting and listening to the Word. Doing without understanding is meaningless. Over and over in the New Testament we have the tension between doing and being, between faith and works. Here, Martha is reminded that actions without love, or taken for the wrong reasons, are not the substance of salvation. It is the Word that saves, and faith that is the avenue to grace. Works are necessary. But they are not enough.

To love God, then, is to sit at the Lord's feet and listen and ponder his every word. It is the balance of the activism of the good Samaritan (and, in a different light, Martha), with the meditative attention of Mary that involves her whole heart, mind, and soul. It is significant that in coupling these two stories, Luke has also balanced the sexes. The good Samaritan and Martha serve as the models of what it is to love neighbor, and Mary, in her quiet, loving, and immovable determination to sit at the feet of the Master and listen, is the exemplar of what it is to love God.

Now we turn to the sisters as we find them in the Gospel of John. "Now a certain man was ill, Lazarus of Bethany, the village of Mary and her sister Martha" (11:1). Immediately we notice that Bethany is identified as the village where the sisters live, suggesting that we know the village because we know the sisters. The text adds a further note of explanation, describing a future event and identifying Mary as the one who anointed Jesus with ointment and wiped his feet with her hair (see Jn. 12:1–8). We are told that the brother of these two women, Lazarus, has fallen ill and the sisters have sent to Jesus to come to "he whom you love" (11:3b). The text tells us that Jesus says this illness will not be fatal, but is to reveal the glory of God and lead to the glorification of the Son. It goes on to point out, "Accordingly, though Jesus loved Martha and her sister and Lazarus, after having heard that Lazarus was ill, he stayed two days longer in the place where he was" (11:5–6). John is a gospel of relationship. Love is mentioned thirty-seven times. Yet very few individuals are named as people that Jesus loved. It is the gospel of the "beloved disciple," and the text mentions Jesus' love for this anonymous disciple five times. I find it significant and very interesting that the writer of the gospel identifies the family and describes the Lord's love for them, giving the sisters primacy of place. (When Martha and Mary send for Jesus, they refer to their brother as one whom Jesus loves, but when the text tells us of his love for them, the women are mentioned first.) Only Mary, Martha, and Lazarus are mentioned by name as being loved by Jesus. Women were traditionally identified through their relationships with the men responsible for them, as in "the daughter of," "the mother of," "the wife of," etc. Here, however, Lazarus is the brother of Mary and Martha (not, "they are the sisters of Lazarus"), and Jesus loved Martha and her sister *and* Lazarus. His disciples are alarmed when Jesus intends to return to the vicinity of Jerusalem, where he is in grave danger from the Jews. Jesus tells them that Lazarus is dead, and that this will present another occasion on which they may "believe." With a stout show of loyalty and courage, Thomas (who later will refuse to believe without solid proof of the resurrection) rallies the disciples to follow Jesus, even if it means all their deaths. Jesus arrives in Bethany after Lazarus has already been in the tomb for four days. The *New Oxford Study Bible* tells us in a footnote that the four days is significant because "popular belief imagined that the soul lingered near the body for three days, then left."[2]

With great consistency of character, it is Martha, the activist of Luke's story, who, hearing that Jesus is near, goes to meet him. Mary, typically, is waiting in the house, quiet (or, as the KJV says, "sat still in the house"–a very evocative image of a woman praying, waiting, *listening*) while Martha runs out to meet him. Just as in the story in Luke, her first words to him combine a complaint and a demand. In Luke's story, she complains about his not noticing that her sister Mary was not helping her, and demands that he make her do so. In John's story, she complains, "Lord, if you had been here, my brother would not have died" (Jn. 11:21), and demands, "But even now I know that God will give you whatever you ask of him" (22). She is clearly struggling between confusion and faith. She is confused because he didn't come as expected, and so her brother has died. Her intimate relationship with Jesus permits her to speak accusingly to him about her disappointment. But her faith tells her that even now, after Lazarus's death,

Jesus still has power to do something. Martha of Bethany is an angry woman, a passionate woman, and a woman of profound, shining faith.

Jesus then gently questions Martha about that faith, and shares with her his teaching about the nature of salvation. What occupied a central place in the great sermons on the plain and mountain in Luke and Matthew's gospels, here is delivered to a grieving and yet faithful woman. In answer to his statement that her brother will rise again, Martha affirms her belief. But she is talking here about the Pharisaic belief that all will rise on the last day. She does not yet expect anything for this day. Then Jesus says something extraordinary. In all three of the synoptic gospels, Jesus elicits the great confession of faith in a conversation with his disciples, asking them, "Who do people say that I am?" (Mk. 8:27). In each case, Peter is the only one to step up and answer, "You are the Messiah" (Mk. 8:29). Matthew's gospel has the most elaborate telling of this event, including Jesus proclaiming of Peter: "On this rock I will build my church" (Mt. 16:18), and promising him "the keys of the kingdom" (Mt. 16:19). All three accounts finish with Jesus warning the disciples "not to tell anyone" (Mk. 8:30). Yet here, as in the story of the woman at the well, Jesus reveals his identity as the Christ to a woman with another of the "I am" sayings. He pronounces some of the most beautiful words in this poetic gospel: "I am the resurrection and the life," (v. 25) and promises that one who believes in him shall never die. Martha responds by making the complete great confession of faith. Again, she does not expect a miracle in the form of physical resuscitation, but is accepting the truth that those who believe in Jesus "though they die, will live" (v. 25). Sandra M. Schneiders writes:

> It is important to realize that Martha's confession of faith is in no way a response to the sign of the raising of Lazarus. It is a response to the word of Jesus revealing himself as the resurrection and the life. The sign comes after Martha's confession and does not function as a guarantee of her faith but as a crisis for the Jews who have gathered. Martha does not expect the sign any more than the disciples of any time or place can expect physical death to be overcome by a miracle.[3]

Yet Martha clearly does expect something. She challenges Jesus with her knowledge of his power, even as his mother Mary had in turning to Jesus about the wine. When Martha reminds Jesus of what she believes, "But even now I know that God will give you whatever you ask of him" (11:22), she is stating her faith that even the unthinkable is possible for Jesus. Martha may not clearly expect Jesus to roll the stone away, but she is certainly clearing the path to the tomb.

Martha, then, functions in this story as a disciple of great faith. Even in the face of the death of her brother, when she knows Jesus could have healed him had he come in time, her faith in *him* is unshaken.

REFLECTION: Candles of Grace

Well, we've all been in the dark in our lives. We've been in the dark physically, whether hiding in a closet playing "hide and seek," or outside on a moonless night under the whispering trees of a forest. Perhaps you have walked, semi-lost, in that whispering darkness, anxious for a glimmer of light to lead you home—like Portia in Shakespeare's *Merchant of Venice,* who, approaching home from a distance, sees a welcoming candle in a window and comments: "How far that little candle throws his beams! So shines a good deed in a naughty world."[4] Or perhaps you have stood in a cave deep inside the earth, when, as some tourist guides do, they turned out the lights to let you experience perfect, complete darkness. It's as close as we the living can come to the darkness of the tomb while yet we live. If you have had that experience, or one like it, I believe you also celebrated that moment when the flashlight came back on and, following that modern candle of grace, you could obey the command of the guide, to follow and "come out."

Certainly we've all been in the dark, mentally. I say it at least twice a week—"I'm completely in the dark," about something. And I experience the feeling every day. There is so much in life not to understand, not to comprehend; the sheer enormity of confusion is like an avalanche of darkness hovering, threatening to overwhelm and sweep away reason and security and understanding. I don't understand why, in a world where there is abundance of food, people are hungry. I don't understand why there are children without shoes, books, or opportunity. I don't understand the indifference of those with power to change what *is* into what *could be.* I don't understand the human passions to control, condemn, judge, and hate. I don't understand why the universe was created to include death. I don't understand why we as a nation spend unbelievable resources on killing and so much less on healing, so that so many people die before their full potential has been fulfilled. When I contemplate the senseless waste of lives, creativity, and resources by an uncaring humanity, I am completely in the dark. I don't understand the sometimes vast silence of God. And then, someone turns on a flashlight, turns on the porch light, and summons me out of the darkness, calling me home. I think they are the saints of God, and they are here, there, everywhere, working for the kingdom, praying for the kingdom, trusting, loving, caring, building, and lighting candles of grace to cast their beams of hope into the weary, darkened, and naughty world.

The gospel text for this morning is one of the most famous and dramatic stories in the New Testament. It is a story of preparation, a story that readies us to celebrate the death of death, the end of the tyranny of the tomb. It is a story that gives us a foretaste of what is to come, of the triumph of the love of Jesus, and the power of God over the power of death. This is the story in which one who was dead, yet shall live, shall see again the light of life and love, shall shed the garments of the grave and come out. And it is the story of two women. This is the story of two women whose faith in Jesus survived his silence and absence when one they loved lay dying, and whose faith was undimmed by the darkness of the tomb.

You can preach a sermon on so many different elements of the story. You can find power in the passion and activism of Martha, the energetic and duty-ridden sister who, seeing Jesus approach after an inexplicable delay to the sickbed of her brother, rushes down the road. He arrived too late, too late to help, too late to heal, and much too late to comfort. Can't you see her, blood singing in anger, grief, and disappointment? Yet through her rage and sorrow she still finds it possible to affirm her faith that to know Jesus is to somehow be in the presence of hope and to believe in healing. It is to believe that to be in his presence is to be in the presence of the Christ, the Son of God, he who is coming into the world. Where would we be in the church, where would we ever have been, without the example of the fire that fuels her love, the passion that energizes her sense of purpose and mission? Who would have slaved joyfully for the kingdom, sacrificed lives to loving mission, without the example of Martha, the activist, the worker, the caretaker? Martha's blood has flowed through the church since the beginning, always singing in its righteous indignation against injustice and corruption, defying disappointment and complacency, *trusting* in the face of disaster, *claiming* Christ's love and *demanding* its response. How dark the world would have been without the witness of Martha: candle of grace summoning us, calling us to action and to work for the kingdom?

You can preach a sermon on the beautiful contemplative faith of Mary from the next section of chapter 11. How shining her faith, as she falls at the feet of Jesus and also states what to her, as to Martha, is obvious: "Lord, if you had been here, my brother would not have died" (v. 32). Her conviction, her trust in Jesus as the Messiah has shone out of these pages for centuries, lighting the way for all who walk in the darkness of doubt and despair. How would the church have survived, all those centuries, without the faith and hope, without the trust of the mystics, the poets, the artists whose vision was painted in the colors of the Divine, whose hearts were filled with the music of heaven, and whose trust was so perfect that even death could not dim the light by which they walked? How would we endure the constant noise of disaster, the endless repetition of death and destruction we hear and see, without the life of the spirit? How dark the world would be without the undimmed vision of Mary: candle of grace, summoning us to prayer, to thought, to faith.

And, of course, you can preach a sermon about Lazarus—about what it must have been like to wake up in the tomb, everywhere the stench of your own death, the stifling heat, the airlessness of the tomb, and the darkness, dear God, the darkness! Yet in that airless and hopeless darkness, he hears a voice, and though blinded by the darkness of the tomb, he responds, as he must to the voice calling him to "come out, come out into the present; the past is dead and over, and the future is not done with you. Come out into the light where work, effort, hope, sorrow, disappointment, and the necessity of trust still wait for you. Come where the task of living waits for you to take it up again as you must, for you are to be a candle of grace shining in the dark, driving away the dark, burning in the hearts of those to come. The world waits for you to be a lamp, Lazarus, to help lighten the load of despair and confusion, so—come out!"

We in the church must celebrate, revere, and stand in awe of the life witness of those who have lit up the heavens with the greatness of their gifts. We must give thanks for Mother Teresa, who was a lamp in the terrible darkness and suffering of India, a depth of suffering you and I shall surely never know or begin to understand. We must give thanks for the awesome ministry of Martin Luther King Jr., whose greatness of spirit and love, humility, and determination lit beacons of hope for justice for everyone, black and white, and gave us the power to dream. We must also study with profound gratitude the message of Martha, Mary, and Lazarus as they each lit the path for the future believers in need of energy, trust, and acceptance. And we sing praises of those who gave their lives for their beliefs, who died to help others, who lived to build the kingdom. But though we remember the great saints of the church in ancient and modern times, it is also appropriate that we celebrate in the priesthood of all believers those we have known whose voices taught us about love, fidelity, and faith; whose firm and kindly hands urged us on the way and helped us to feel safe; who led us through dark times; and whose memories shine in our thoughts like candles of grace. Perhaps, most important of all, they summon us to lay aside our bandages and our restraints, to abandon the comfortable oblivion of indifference, the tombs of selfishness and greed, to stand up and stand for something bigger and far more important than our own needs and desires.

The church is in dire need of saints, and the ones of the past, towering as they were and continue to be, will not be enough. We need saints now, saints who are willing to step up to the mark laid down by those whose lives have illumined the way. We treasure the reflection of their candles, but we need brave bright lights burning today if we are to find our way out of the darkness of these times. Church attendance is falling, membership crumbling in every denomination. Voices in pulpits across the country and, indeed, the world, are growing ever more strident as they list those who are evil, those who are abomination, those who must be held down, suppressed, punished, and cast out. Christianity, the very term, has been hijacked by hate mongers, by people masquerading as Christians who yet seem totally unacquainted with the message of the Jesus life as it is given us in the gospels. This man, this Jesus—the greatest candle of grace, the light of the world—this man who shunned publicity and honor, who abandoned worldly goods and wealth, who elected to live simply and found the humility to accept hospitality and care from others; this man who loved everyone extravagantly and condemned no one, whose message was of a loving God, a living God, a God who was to us like a father giving good things to his children, a mother sheltering her young under her wings; this man Jesus whose entire ministry shunned the power structures of life and religious institutions; this is the man in whose name hatred and prejudice and judgment are pronounced by fundamentalists and institutional churches everywhere. What on earth would Jesus say if he could see what has been done in his name? Not just the atrocities committed against those of different ideas, the Inquisitions and the purges and the executions for heresy—those terrors would sadden and horrify him sure enough. But I believe he would be just as angry, just as appalled, at the addiction to power and hierarchy churches have foisted upon his name; the power structures more concerned with subjugating and controlling people than with feeding, comforting, and enlightening them. I believe he would reject absolutely those who, in his name, promote hatred of women, of gay and lesbian persons, of those whose understandings of theology are different and challenging, of anyone who prizes the power of reason and freedom, rejecting those who would put braces on our brains and blow out all the candles of new ideas and understanding. We need saints today to stand up and stand against that kind of narrowness of vision that would foist darkness upon the rest of us. We need to think of ourselves as lamps and candles, as saints in God's kingdom, because that, my dear friends, is what we are, each and every one, called to be.

Each of us is called to be a candle of grace for those we know, and for those who come after. We must reclaim what we know to be Christian from the encroaching darkness. We must stand for justice, inclusiveness, forgiveness, and the complete assurance of the extravagant love of God. We must break open the tombs that imprison the human spirit—ignorance, prejudice, and parochialism—by rolling away the stones. And we must call out to each cowering soul longing for the life-giving light of God's love and human acceptance as one of the family of God, longing for the touch of a helping compassionate hand, longing for the promise of freedom and understanding, longing for the candles of grace to light their path, "Come out!"

Notes

[1]Quoted in Leonard Swidler, "Jesus Was a Feminist," *Catholic World* (January, 1971): 178.

[2]Herbert G. May and Bruce M. Metzger, eds., *The New Oxford Annotated Bible with the Apocrypha, Revised Standard Version* (New York: Oxford University Press, 1979), 1304.

[3]Sandra Schneiders, *Written That You May Believe: Encountering Jesus in the Fourth Gospel* (New York: Crossroad, 1999), 106.

[4]William Shakespeare, *The Merchant of Venice,* Act v., Scene 1.

Why Has My Lord Not Come To Me?

O Martha dear, o sister strong,
Bring close your candle to my face.
The dark denies all power of light,
And cold withholds your warm embrace.
Now send, oh send, word to his ear,
The one you love so longs to see,
The promise of your living word,
Why does my Lord not come to me?

O Mary sister, o dearest one,
Hold tight my hand beside my bed,
And let your prayers fall on my ear
As one from whom all hope has fled.
Now call, oh call him to my side,
Let not my sorrow endless be,
as silence grows, my heart despairs,
Why has my Lord not come to me?

The silence full, the dark complete
No thought, no breath disturbs my tomb,
And who could know that solid stone
Would soon become a life-bearing womb?
Now has the darkness released its hold,
My spirit from all graves set free,
My Lord stands calling to all of God's children,
Come now dear friend, come out to me.

Words by Judith Jones
Tune: Traditional Scottish Melody, "Candler"

5

New Discipleship

Six days before the Passover Jesus came to Bethany, the home of Lazarus, whom he had raised from the dead. There they gave a dinner for him. Martha served, and Lazarus was one of those at the table with him. Mary took a pound of costly perfume made of pure nard, anointed Jesus' feet, and wiped them with her hair. The house was filled with the fragrance of the perfume. But Judas Iscariot, one of his disciples (the one who was about to betray him), said, "Why was this perfume not sold for three hundred *denarii* and the money given to the poor?" (He said this not because he cared about the poor, but because he was a thief; he kept the common purse and used to steal what was put into it.) Jesus said, "Leave her alone. She bought it so that she might keep it for the day of my burial. You always have the poor with you, but you do not always have me." (Jn. 12:1–8)

The story of the anointing of Jesus by Mary of Bethany is anticipated at the beginning of the previous story of Martha and the raising of Lazarus. "Mary was the one who anointed the Lord with perfume and wiped his feet with her hair; her brother Lazarus was ill" (Jn. 11:2). This insertion points to the extreme importance of this act, so important that it is critical even in the astonishing story of the raising of Lazarus, to clarify who Mary really is. Again we are at the home of Martha and her sister Mary and, as in the story in Luke, there is a meal underway. Lazarus is seated at the table with Jesus, but he is only mentioned as present. He neither speaks nor acts, nor is spoken to by others. With lovely consistency, we are told "Martha served," using the Greek verb *diakonein,* which is the word from which we derive "diaconate" and "deacon." Sandra Schneiders points out that by the time John's gospel was written, this word had become a liturgical term of ministry in some Christian communities.[1] Clearly, Martha was a symbol of the hospitality and service required of those who follow Christ. Just as clearly, she was recognized as fulfilling the role of minister.

The story focuses on Mary and her act of anointing Jesus. This text is perhaps the most responsible for the confusion of Mary of Bethany with the sinful woman from Luke's gospel and with Mary Magdalene. There is an anointing story in all three of the synoptic gospels. Mark, the earliest of the gospels, tells us that an anointing took place at Bethany, though in the house of Simon the leper: "As he sat at the table, a woman came with an alabaster jar of very costly ointment of nard, and she broke open the jar and poured the ointment on his head" (Mk. 14:3). Some of those present decried this extravagance, saying it should have been sold and used to help the poor, but they are not named. Jesus defends the unnamed woman by saying:

> "Let her alone; why do you trouble her? She has performed a good service for me. For you always have the poor with you, and you can show kindness to them whenever you wish; but you will not always have me. She has done what she could; she has anointed my body beforehand for its burial. Truly I tell you, wherever the good news is proclaimed in the whole world, what she has done will be told in remembrance of her" (Mark 14:6b–9).

Matthew's version (Mt. 26:6–13) is very similar. The anointing reminds us that the Old Testament prophets anointed kings by pouring oil over their heads. In these two stories, the woman performs this solemn and reverent act, and the kingship of Jesus is evoked at the same time as the funeral rite of anointing. Her hair is not mentioned, and this is important because a woman's hair was then, as now, her "crowning glory," and respectable women kept their heads covered when out in public. Only in Luke 7:36–50 is the woman identified as a sinner, a woman of the town. The sinful woman does not pour the oil on Jesus' head, but instead kisses Jesus' feet, bathes them with her tears and anoints them with the expensive oil. It is her humility and penitence, rather than her reverence, that are highlighted. Both Mark and Matthew place the story immediately before Judas' betrayal and the last supper with the disciples. In both of these versions, Jesus goes to that communion meal anointed for his burial. Luke's story comes at a different point. He places it early in the ministry of Jesus and in the midst of a teaching section, immediately following, "The Son of Man has come eating and drinking, and you say, 'Look, a glutton and a drunkard, a friend of tax collectors and sinners!'" (Lk. 7:34). Luke uses the sinful woman and her gift to point up the stinginess of the meal's host, and as a teaching about forgiveness. The sinful woman becomes a paradigm for the repentant sinner who, because she has shown great love, has been forgiven for her many sins. The story closes with Jesus promising the woman salvation because of her faith.

John's anointing story is again placed just before Jesus' return to Jerusalem for his last Passover. However, unlike that of the synoptic gospels, his last meal with the disciples after he returns to Jerusalem will not be the Passover meal itself, and it has a very different focus than the consecration of bread and wine in Christ's name. That focus is symbolized in the story of the meal in the home of Martha, Mary, and Lazarus. John takes care to ascribe the anointing to Mary of Bethany, who is clearly not a woman of the town, and has never been mentioned as being a sinner. She does, however, appear with her hair unbound, and like the sinful woman of Luke's Gospel, she anoints Jesus' feet and dries them with her hair. It is this detail that caused her to be identified with the sinful woman of that story. It is an unusual detail. Although it is Mary's home, and she would be able to be less formal than if she were in someone else's house, it would still be unusual for a woman to uncover her hair in the presence of guests. Women were not supposed to speak to, much less touch, men who were not members of their families. Mary's act of wiping Jesus' feet with her hair is hard to understand in light of the behavior expected of respectable women. Some have, as described above, explained it by assuming Mary of Bethany is the sinful woman. Others see in it an outpouring of extravagant love and reverence that could only be expressed in a radical and extravagant manner.

Fascination with Dan Brown's novel *The Da Vinci Code* and all things pertaining to the legends of Mary Magdalene has led some enthusiasts to assume that Mary of Bethany must have been intimately related to Jesus to have performed such an act. According to them, since the most interesting of the legends contends that Mary Magdalene was married to Jesus, and since there was a historic coupling of Mary Magdalene and Mary of Bethany dating back to the sixth century (Pope Gregory's sermon on Luke), clearly Mary's action was that of a grieving and loving wife. Unfortunately for the romantics, it is not really that clear. Though her behavior was certainly unorthodox for women of her time, the entire gospel of John presents women doing things that were considered unorthodox. Women did not converse with men, still less with rabbis in public. Yet the woman at the well did so and held her own with wit and aplomb. Women did not sit at the feet of rabbis and listen to teaching, yet Mary of Bethany did so in the companion story from Luke's gospel, and nothing about the story truly suggests that this was unusual behavior for her. The most likely reason for her act, in my opinion, is her deep love and respect for her teacher and Lord who had opened the world of the mind to her, as well as that of the heart and spirit. The washing of the feet and anointing with oil was a hospitable act, though normally performed by a slave. Mary is Jesus' disciple, and here she yet again claims for herself the privilege of ministering to him as a disciple, in a beautiful and powerful way. She demonstrates here the humility of one who, as a true disciple, is willing to be a slave for Christ.

The gospel of John is very clear that it was the raising of Lazarus from the dead that precipitated the plot to kill Jesus (and Lazarus as well). For the other gospels, it is generally believed that it was the cleansing of the temple that led to his arrest. This puts the two stories about Mary, Martha, and Lazarus at the very heart of the gospel, at the moment of extreme and imminent danger. The sacrifice of the eucharist is foreshadowed, and the raising up and glorification of Jesus just a heartbeat away.

Following this meal at Bethany, when Mary has demonstrated her understanding of the real situation regarding Jesus and his impending death, we have the meal at which Jesus washes the feet of his disciples. Overcoming Peter's unwillingness, Jesus explains to the disciples that his example of servanthood is the model they must follow:

> After he had washed their feet, had put on his robe, and had returned to the table, he said to them, "Do you know what I have done to you? You call me Teacher and Lord—and you are right, for that is what I am. So if I, your Lord and Teacher, have washed your feet, you also ought to wash one another's feet. For I have set you an example, that you also should do as I have done to you." (Jn. 13:12–15)

This act of foot washing exists in this gospel in the place where the sacrament of the Lord's supper exists in the synoptics. This is the profound gift Jesus gives to his followers, the gift of humility and servanthood. Mary of Bethany, who both performs the service of loving disciple and assists Jesus in preparing for his final hour, has modeled that gift in the preceding chapter.

REFLECTION: The Fragrance of Humility

Jesus is almost at the gates of Jerusalem, the end of the journey. He is in the little town of Bethany, across a valley from Jerusalem. He has come to stay with his beloved friends: Lazarus, Mary, and Martha. And gathered at that table were his disciples and his friend Lazarus—Lazarus, the man who had died, cut off from life in one of those "tragic—but what can you do?" kind of things. But something was different about that death—*several* things, actually, beginning with the response of the sisters. In this time people were resigned to death as a frequent, almost inevitable consequence of serious illness. Medicine was primitive, guided by superstition, and certainly what medical knowledge and treatment did exist was not available to the poor or ordinary person. Martha, identified as a person of property, might have summoned doctors, though the text is specific—she summons Jesus. Mary and Martha did not fold their hands in resignation when Lazarus fell ill, they did not just give up and give in and say there was, after all, nothing they could do. There was something they could do and they did it—they sent for Jesus. Jesus, whom they had seen heal others, Jesus who had taught in their house, allowing them to listen, if they liked—you remember, Mary liked! Martha scolded, but that's another story. They sent for him, and Martha demanded explanations for his tardiness. Yet her faith elicited those most glorious words: "Jesus said to her, 'I am the resurrection and the life. Those who believe in me, even though they die, will live, and everyone who lives and believes in me will never die'" (Jn. 11:25). And before their tear-filled eyes, he caused the tomb to be opened and demanded that Lazarus, dead, now alive, should come out and rejoin the living.

Here they are, then, this extraordinary company gathered at the table, a thanksgiving feast, a meal prepared in love and gratitude and unspeakable awe for the miracle, still new and unbearable in its potential meaning—a group of friends eating and drinking together. Jesus is in the midst of them, alone in his understanding, or so it seems. All through the gospel Jesus has understood about the end of the journey, but for the others the end was hidden from their eyes, hidden by their own lack of faith, their inability to face the truth. Here, they must have argued, is one for whom the inevitability of suffering, for whom resignation to evil and death, is unnecessary. He walks on water; he multiplies crumbs into loaves and spreads a banquet in the wilderness for the hungry. He is not resigned to death, for he opens tombs and calls the dead back to the living. For him, death is not inevitable, nor suffering unavoidable. The world isn't like that, for him. They may have thought that, perhaps, because we love him, it isn't like that for us either. No, the disciples did not want to face the end of the road, and in a strange way their unwillingness to confront the end may have been a kind of faith—the belief that Jesus would triumph over suffering and death on his own behalf, as he had so often on behalf of others. They did not understand what lies at the heart of John's gospel.

How lonely Jesus must have felt, as he sat at that table! Then, the extraordinary thing happens. Mary, the quiet one, the one who sat at his feet loving him, listening to him, and treasuring her discipleship, Mary comes into the room with her flask of expensive perfume and proceeds to create consternation. Mary breaks open the flask, this costly luxury item that could have been sold for a huge sum of money, worth a workingman's wages for a year, and pours the valuable ointment on Jesus' feet.

Washing the feet of a guest, and offering perfume (no doubt a lesser quality and certainly a smaller quantity) was an act of hospitality on the part of a gracious host. Yet it would have been performed before the meal, and by a servant. Here we have Mary, her long hair uncovered and unbound, kneeling at the feet of Jesus and squandering a fortune in perfume over his feet, drying them with her hair. Judas, apparently appalled at the extravagance, complains. The gospel writer lets us know that Judas' concern for the poor is false, but for the others it must have seemed like serious, conspicuous consumption. And Jesus, in answer to their surprise and criticism, says this amazing thing: "The poor you always have with you. But I am with you only for a little while longer. She is preparing me for my burial" (vv. 7–8, paraphrased).

At first glance, it must appear that Jesus is voicing the resignation of the world: The poor are always there. You cannot save them, you cannot really help with your well-meaning but puny efforts, so never mind about them. But that is not the meaning of the passage. We have too many times heard Jesus take on the establishment way of thinking to believe for a moment that he is in any way resigned to poverty as inescapable, inevitable, or normal. Everywhere along his journey he found time to comfort, to heal, to flout the conventions of the time, and even to break the law in order to alleviate the suffering of the poor. No, Jesus was not expressing resignation for the poor. He was expressing his appreciation, his gratitude for the deep understanding and sacrifice of one of the little ones, of Mary, on his behalf. He, the giver of so much compassion and so many gifts of healing and help, he was receiving a lavish outpouring of love and generosity, an attempt to comfort him on the eve of his great and final sacrifice of which this costly squandering was but a tiny foretelling.

Mary was not resigned. She did not fold her hands, and say, "Oh well, it's God's will, can't be helped, it's the way of the world." She saw someone in need, someone in pain, and she reached deep into her resources for the absolute best she possessed. She gave not stingily, not carefully or conservatively, but lavishly in her efforts to comfort. She gave a gift of surpassing generosity so that Jesus might feel loved, cherished, companioned on his journey. It was a breathtaking gift of love and worship.

We are in a world that seems on every hand to be against the love of God. We see indifferent governments cutting humanitarian programs, we see fewer and fewer resources devoted to protecting the helpless, feeding the hungry, healing the sick, reconciling the disenfranchised, or liberating the oppressed. We can sit on our hands and say, "Yes, that's too bad–a tragedy. But that is the way it is. I can't do anything." Or we can say, as did Mary, "I can do something. I can reach out to this suffering one and give the best I can to make it better. I can give a real gift of love and sacrifice so that one other person in this life will know the meaning of the good news." Mary was, of course, fortunate. She was giving her gift directly to Jesus. She was soothing the suffering of the Christ. Where would we find Jesus to minister to, after all? Where would we find the suffering Christ to receive our gifts of love and compassion and sacrifice? Why, *everywhere*.

Notes

[1]Sandra Schneiders, *Written That You May Believe: Encountering Jesus in the Fourth Gospel* (New York: Crossroad, 1999), 107. "By the time John's Gospel was written at the end of the first century the term diakonos, 'servant,' had become the title of a recognized ministerial office in some Christian communities (see Phil. 1:1; 1 Tim. 3:8, 13; Rom. 16:1), and waiting on table a function conferred by the laying on of hands (Acts 6:1–6)."

6

Another Beginning

Meanwhile, standing near the cross of Jesus were his
mother, and his mother's sister, Mary the wife of
Clopas, and Mary Magdalene. When Jesus saw his mother
and the disciple whom he loved standing beside her, he said
to his mother, "Woman, here is your son." Then he said to the
disciple, "Here is your mother." And from that hour the disciple
took her into his own home. (Jn. 19:25b–27)

On the terrifying hill of Golgotha, the place of the skull, we meet the
mother of Jesus again. If we see the miracle at Cana as the birth of Jesus'
earthly ministry, this is the story of its conclusion. But even as it is a narrative
of death, this is also a birth story. If we look at the story, we see several
similarities with the miracle at Cana. In the Cana story we noted that Mary
is mentioned first, even before Jesus and his disciples, giving added weight
to the importance of her presence. Here, following the mention of Jesus
on his cross, the witnesses are named, and his mother is listed first. Mary
Magdalene also is mentioned, and in this detail alone this passion narrative
is synchronous with the synoptic gospels, all three of which name Mary
Magdalene as present. John alone, however, mentions Mary, the mother
of Jesus. The second mention of the mother of Jesus is in company with
another iconic figure present, the beloved disciple, and the mother of Jesus
is again mentioned first, emphasizing her importance.

Jesus addresses his mother in exactly he same way he did at Cana,
calling her "woman." There can be no question here that this is not a
discourteous form of address, nor that it expresses any annoyance on Jesus'
part, as has often been suggested about his use of it in the Cana story. In
both cases her importance is greater than the fact that she is his mother,

and the use of "woman" rather than a more familiar way of speaking to her emphasizes her iconic role.

Jesus then commits his mother and the Beloved Disciple into one another's care, and it should be noted that he commits the disciple to the care of his mother first. Much has been written about this adoption and its meaning. It has been used to bolster the idea of Mary's perpetual virginity, for, the argument goes, if she truly had other sons and daughters, she would not need to be given into the care of someone outside her family. I believe that the synoptics tell us she had sons and daughters, and the story here is not about physical custody of and responsibility for Jesus' mother. This story is about a much larger relationship.[1] Many scholars believe that Mary here represents the church, and the beloved disciple all those Christians who, upon believing, become brothers and sisters of Jesus, children of God. Raymond Brown, in his commentary of the gospel of John for the Anchor Bible series[2] points to the later use of mother and birth imagery in this gospel: "In becoming the mother of the Beloved Disciple (the Christian), Mary is symbolically evocative of Lady Zion who, after the birth pangs, brings forth a new people in joy."[3] This assertion explains Jesus' teachings on the subject:

> "Very truly, I tell you, you will weep and mourn, but the world will rejoice; you will have pain, but your pain will turn into joy. When a woman is in labor, she has pain, because her hour has come. But when her child is born, she no longer remembers the anguish because of the joy of having brought a human being into the world. So you have pain now; but I will see you again, and your hearts will rejoice, and no one will take your joy from you" (Jn. 16:20–22).

Another pointer to the relationship of these two stories, Cana and the cross, is the use of the word "hour." In the Cana story, when Mary points out the lack of wine, Jesus demurs from involving himself in the problem because, as he says, "My hour has not yet come." From the cross Jesus commits the beloved disciple to his mother's care, and his mother to the care of the disciple, and "from that hour the disciple took her to his own home" (Jn. 19:27). The word "hour" was used to describe the time of labor to bring forth a child, and the pain associated with that process. Jesus has also used it throughout the gospel to describe the hour of his sacrifice as he labors in death on the cross to give birth to the promise of eternal life and salvation. The use of it here calls the birth process to mind and also suggests Mary as the mother of Jesus, the mother of his ministry, and the mother of the church.[4]

Finally, both stories refer to the symbols of water and wine. In the gospel of John, water represents the spiritual birth and fulfillment Christians find through faith in Jesus Christ. Wine is inescapably linked in the mind of

Christians with the passion and Christ's blood, shed for the sins of many. The wine at Cana foreshadows Christ's blood on Calvary. Water, living water, is always the water of baptism through which the believer dies to the old life of the world and is reborn in the spirit. At birth, both water and blood signify a new being coming into the world. At Cana, water and wine that is also blood signify the birth of Jesus' ministry. At Calvary, when a soldier pierces Jesus' side, water and blood flow out , signifying the birth of the Church and the new life into which all Christians are born. New children of God are coming into the world through the salvation of the cross.

The mother of Jesus only appears in these two stories in the gospel of John. Her presence at the beginning and at the end of Jesus' ministry encompasses all the teaching of Jesus, and all the miracle stories save only the resurrection. She is his first disciple, believing before the other disciples, before the miracle at Cana, and confident that whatever he does will be doing the will of God. At Calvary she is still one of the most faithful. Only she, the other women, and the shadowy figure of the beloved disciple have not deserted Jesus in his hour of being lifted up. Mary the mother of Jesus was the first to see the light, and is faithful to her vision and her love even to death. With beautiful symmetry she has walked the entire journey from Cana to the cross, faithful to the end.[5]

REFLECTION: New Birth

How agonizing it must have been for a mother to stand there at the foot of that terrible instrument of torture and death, watching the slow suffering of her beloved son. How unimaginable to stand there and watch him die. Yet her faith keeps her there, steadfast and courageous until the end. She embodies the sorrow and anguish of every woman who has to watch, helpless, as her child dies in this unjust and uncaring world.

This is no distant, sweet and passive woman. This is a woman of magnificent energy, of vision and determination, who fully embraced life with love and passion and courage. This is a woman who, there at the last moments of his life, is in her son's heart. As he died, Jesus commended his beloved disciple to her care: "Woman, behold your (new) son; friend, beloved disciple, behold your (new) mother" (vv. 26–27, paraphrased). In Acts we will see Mary at the heart of the church in Jerusalem with the disciples, constantly praying, the heartbeat of the new church. She was a woman who did not accept the dictates of her society. She was a woman who, unmarried, accepted the burden and danger and shame of being an unmarried mother, taking God's word that she would be the mother of the Savior of the world. She was a woman who did not always understand, but still pursued with faith and courage to be a support to her son, to express her love and strength in what must have been a bewildering series of events.

She was a woman who loved passionately, believed passionately, and who, clearly declining to pine away in her grief after the death of her son, was a leader in the new church, the mother of the new church, which would grow and change the world.

She is steadfast in the face of death, faithful when there was despair all around, never sitting passively but rather leading the new church by modeling her faith and her strength. Mary, the mother of Jesus, was the perfect disciple from the beginning, whenever we count that beginning to be. She was courageous in the face of angelic announcements and labor and birth in a stable, proclaiming the radical new order of all things, the mighty brought low and the poor and powerless lifted up (see Lk. 1:52). She brought him up to see women in a respectful and caring way; teaching, worrying about, and loving her son as he grew, speaking the truth fearlessly and forcefully, questioning, challenging, and supporting—and always, always faithful.

Women of the church, go and do likewise.

Notes

[1]Raymond E. Brown, *The Gospel According to John XIII–XXI, The Anchor Bible* (New York: Doubleday, 1970), 925.

"Setting aside the apologetic and popular developments, we doubt that Jesus' filial solicitude is the main import of the Johannine scene. Such a non-theological interpretation would make this episode a misfit amid the highly symbolic episodes that surround it in the crucifixion narrative. Moreover, the Gospel gives several indications that something more profound is in mind. The wording 'Here is your son' and 'Here is your mother' is another instance of the revelatory formula that De Goedt has detected elsewhere in John (vol. 29, p. 58). In this formula the one who speaks is revealing the mystery of the special salvific mission that the one referred to will undertake; thus, the sonship and motherhood proclaimed from the cross are of value for God's plan and are related to what is being accomplished in the elevation of Jesus on the cross. A deeper meaning is also suggested by the verse that follows this episode in John: 'After this, [Jesus was] aware that all was now finished.' The action of Jesus in relation to his mother and the Beloved Disciple completes the work that the father has given Jesus to do and fulfills the Scripture (see Note on 'in order to' in xix 28). All this implies something more profound than filial care (although, if the scene is historical, filial care may have been its original import)."

[2]Ibid., 925.

[3]Ibid.

[4]Gerard Sloyan, *John,* Interpretation: A Bible Commentary for Teaching and Preaching (Atlanta: John Knox Press, 1988), 211. Sloyan alludes to this role as mother of the church when he writes: "John has three women—or four or two depending on how one punctuates—'standing by the cross.' Of these, Jesus' mother is the one John uses for a typological purpose. Along with the 'disciple whom he loved' the women stand near. The 'woman' (cf. 2:4) is given over to her anonymous adoptive son and this son to his new mother. He takes her 'to his own' (v. 27), a pregnant phrase because identical with that used by Jesus to describe the scattering of his disciples who would leave him quite alone (16:32), each gone 'to his own.' Jesus as Word had, at the very outset, come *eis ta idia* and *hoi idioi* had not received him (1:11). Now a spiritual son reverses that tragic history and receives a mother from 'the Son,' to begin a community of believers in that only Son who speaks with power from the cross."

It should be noted, however, that Sloyan does as many interpreters do, in that he describes Jesus as giving his mother to the beloved disciple, while I think it is significant that he begins with the giving of the disciple to his mother.

[5]In her thoughtful writing about the women in the gospel of John, Sandra M. Schneiders chooses not to include Mary, because she believes her femaleness is irrelevant to her primary argument: "The theological reason for excluding the material about the mother of Jesus from this study is that the femaleness of Mary as she is presented in the Fourth Gospel, although historically factual and symbolically important, is irrelevant for the issue under discussion here, namely, the Gospel's contribution to our imaging of women believers as women. First, it is obvious that the mother of Jesus, unlike his interlocutors in Samaria, at Bethany, or in the garden of the tomb, could not have been other than female. Second, whatever role Mary is assigned in the Fourth Gospel, it is either unique to her or universal, in neither of which cases is it more significant for women than for men." While I agree with this argument with regard to Mary's being a universal symbol, I believe that her femaleness is of significant importance in the structure of the gospel of John. Because of the role women play in this gospel, the femaleness of Mary, even if she is the mother of Jesus and therefore unique and at the same time universal, does speak powerfully to the role women must have played in the Johannine community and their understanding of the role women played in the life of Jesus. If women are, as I believe, the supporting bone structure of the ministry of Jesus as presented in this gospel, then Mary is the first and final vertebra of that ministry.

7

New Life

Early on the first day of the week, while it was still dark, Mary Magdalene came to the tomb and saw that the stone had been removed from the tomb. So she ran and went to Simon Peter and the other disciple, the one whom Jesus loved, and said to them, "They have taken the Lord out of the tomb, and we do not know where they have laid him." Then Peter and the other disciple set out and went toward the tomb. The two were running together, but the other disciple outran Peter and reached the tomb first. He bent down to look in and saw the linen wrappings lying there, but he did not go in. Then Simon Peter came, following him, and went into the tomb. He saw the linen wrappings lying there, and the cloth that had been on Jesus' head, not lying with the linen wrappings but rolled up in a place by itself. Then the other disciple, who reached the tomb first, also went in, and he saw and believed; for as yet they did not understand the scripture, that he must rise from the dead. Then the disciples returned to their homes.

But Mary stood weeping outside the tomb. As she wept, she bent over to look into the tomb; and she saw two angels in white, sitting where the body of Jesus had been lying, one at the head and the other at the feet. They said to her, "Woman, why are you weeping?" She said to them, "They have taken away my Lord, and I do not know where they have laid him." When she had said this, she turned around and saw Jesus standing there, but she did not know that it was Jesus. Jesus said to her, "Woman, why are you weeping? Whom are you looking for?" Supposing him to be the gardener, she said to him, "Sir, if you

have carried him away, tell me where you have laid him, and I
will take him away." Jesus said to her, "Mary!" She turned and
said to him in Hebrew, "Rabbouni!" (which means Teacher).
Jesus said to her, "Do not hold on to me, because I have not
yet ascended to the Father. But go to my brothers and say to
them, 'I am ascending to my Father and your Father, to my God
and your God.'" Mary Magdalene went and announced to the
disciples, "I have seen the Lord"; and she told them that he had
said these things to her. (Jn. 20:1–18)

Many of us grew up "knowing" quite a lot about Mary Magdalene.
We "knew" she was a prostitute. So prevalent has that idea been that,
in nineteenth-century England, a woman who became a prostitute was
said to have entered "the Magdalene." We "knew" that she repented of
her sins and that she came and knelt at Jesus' feet, bathing his feet with
her penitent tears and drying them with her hair. Hundreds of artists
have portrayed her as a beautiful woman with long red hair, holding an
ointment jar, symbolizing the costly perfume she used to anoint the Lord's
feet. Donatello's magnificent gilded wood sculpture of Mary Magdalene,
carved c. 1453–55, is entitled *The Penitent Magdalene,*[1] as are countless other
sculptures and paintings.

In fact, all of these things are inaccurate, based on mistakes, legends,
misogyny, and the popular imagination–but not on the scriptural account.
So much has been written about Mary Magdalene in recent years, fiction
and pseudo-fact and serious scholarly thought, that it has become harder to
separate legend from knowledge. The powerful persistence of legend is clear
when we consider that the identification of Mary Magdalene as a prostitute,
as well as with Mary of Bethany and the sinful woman from the gospel
of Luke, occurred in the sixth century due to a pronouncement by Pope
Gregory the Great.[2] This identification persists in the popular imagination
despite the Vatican's repudiation (albeit somewhat quietly) of this notion
in 1969, separating Mary of Magdala from Mary of Bethany, and from the
sinful woman in Luke. Centuries of tradition, profound devotion to this
icon of sinner, penitent, forgiven, and redeemed, and countless magnificent
artistic representations have imbedded the idea too deeply in the public
consciousness to be easily transformed.

What do the scriptures actually tell us about Mary Magdalene? In
order to understand John's portrayal of her, we must first look at her as
described in the other gospel narratives. To begin with the earliest gospel,
Mark, does not mention her until the passion, where he names her as
present at the crucifixion, "looking on from a distance," accompanied by
"Mary the mother of James the younger and of Joses, and Salome. These
used to follow him and provided for him when he was in Galilee; and there
were many other women who had come up with him to Jerusalem" (Mk.

15:40–41). He goes on to place her at the tomb. "Mary Magdalene and Mary the mother of Joses saw where the body was laid" (Mk. 15:47). Later, "When the sabbath was over, Mary Magdalene, and Mary the mother of James, and Salome bought spices, so that they might go and anoint him. And very early on the first day of the week, when the sun had risen, they went to the tomb" (Mk. 16:1–2). The women find the stone rolled away from the tomb, and an angel, or young man dressed in white, who tells them that Jesus has been raised. Though he tells them to go and tell Peter and the disciples that Jesus is going to meet them in Galilee, the women are too terrified to do so and they tell no one. Most of the oldest versions of Mark's gospel end there, though one authority concludes with a short passage in which the women do tell the disciples what they had seen and heard. A longer ending, added at a later time, has one more reference to Mary Magdalene:

> Now after he rose early on the first day of the week, he appeared first to Mary Magdalene, from whom he had cast out seven demons. She went out and told those who had been with him, while they were mourning and weeping. But when they heard that he was alive and had been seen by her, they would not believe it. (from the "Longer Ending," Mk. 16:9–11)

Therefore, we know from the earliest version of the story in Mark's gospel that Mary Magdalene was present at the cross, though at a distance; that she followed the removal of Jesus' body and saw where it was laid; that after the Sabbath she returned to the tomb with spices to anoint his body; that she is confronted by an angelic presence who tells her Jesus has risen and commissions her to go and tell Peter and the disciples; but that she (and the other women with her) were too terrified to do so at first. At least one manuscript, however, concludes that the women did finally share their witness as they had been commanded to do. It is not until the later, longer ending that Mary Magdalene is identified as one from whom Jesus "had cast out seven demons" (Mk. 16:9). It is noticeable that this added remark appears to be there to identify her, but Mark's earlier mention of her at the cross has already identified her as one of the women who helped to financially support Jesus.

Matthew's gospel follows the pattern of the earliest Markan text, introducing Mary Magdalene at the cross, and also as being among the women who had "followed Jesus from Galilee and had provided for him" (Mt. 27:55b). She and the other Mary are there to locate the tomb, and return after the Sabbath. There is no mention of spices or of their intention to anoint the body of Jesus. They also encounter an angel who descends from heaven and rolls the stone away from the tomb. I simply must point out here the lovely irony of what follows. The (presumably) large, strong guards Matthew places outside the tomb faint in terror at the sight of the angelic visitor, but the two women heroically stand fast and listen to the message of resurrection. Then Matthew tells us, "So they left the tomb quickly with fear and great joy, and ran to tell his disciples. Suddenly Jesus met them and said, 'Greetings!' And they came to him, took hold of his feet, and worshiped him. Then Jesus said to them, 'Do not be afraid: go and tell my brothers to go to Galilee; there they will see me'" (Mt. 28:8–10). Matthew reiterates the information that Mary Magdalene was one of those women of substance who helped support Jesus, but makes no mention of her having been possessed by demons or in any other way infirm. Matthew does not have the two women paralyzed with fear, but joyfully running with the good news, and apparently their message was powerful and convincing, because the disciples went to Galilee to meet Jesus as instructed.

Luke's gospel is the only one to mention Mary Magdalene outside of the passion narratives. Luke tells us:

> Soon afterwards he went on through cities and villages, proclaiming and bringing the good news of the kingdom of God. The twelve were with him, as well as some women who had been cured of evil spirits and infirmities: Mary, called Magdalene, from whom seven demons had gone out, and Joanna, the wife of Herod's steward Chuza, and Susanna, and many others, who provided for them out of their resources. (Lk. 8:1–3)

Luke again mentions her in his passion narrative, although she is first presumably among "all his acquaintances, including the women who had followed him from Galilee" (Lk. 23:49). Luke describes the women locating the tomb, and returning with spices following the Sabbath. They encounter not one but two angelic visitors in dazzling clothes, and Luke's version has the women terrified, and bowing their faces to the ground. When they go as instructed and tell the disciples, they are not believed by anyone except Peter, who runs to the tomb and is amazed at what he finds—or does not find—there.

To summarize the appearance of Mary Magdalene in the synoptic gospels, Luke and Mark (though only in the later, added ending) mention that she had been cured of seven demons, but Matthew says nothing about it. She appears in all three gospels during the passion narrative and is placed at the cross, and later at the tomb. All three gospels tell us she encountered an angelic visitor (or two), who in the synoptics proclaimed to her and her companions the good news and sent them all to tell the disciples. All three describe Mary Magdalene as a woman of substance who, along with others, supported Jesus and his ministry out of their own personal wealth.

Now we turn to the gospel of John. John tells us, unlike the synoptic versions, that Mary Magdalene—along with three or four other women, including the Lord's mother (the number may be read differently, according to punctuation)—stood *near* the cross (Jn. 19:25b), unlike the synoptic stories, which place them at a distance. The relative distance to the cross is important, because, in John's gospel, Jesus speaks to his mother from there. The focus in this passage is on Jesus, his mother and the beloved disciple, who somehow appears after the original description of who is standing near. John's version continues to diverge from the synoptic texts. She is unaccompanied—only Mary Magdalene is mentioned as coming to the tomb. She goes to the disciples without being sent by angels, and describes the empty tomb and her fear that the body of Jesus has been stolen. Peter and the beloved disciple run to the tomb, and in a somewhat contradictory manner we are told the beloved disciple "saw and believed"; yet following that, the text tells us "for as yet they did not understand the scripture, that he must rise from the dead" (Jn. 20:8b–9). *What* the beloved disciple believed is therefore unclear, as it was apparently not that Jesus had risen.

The two disciples then leave the tomb. Mary remains, weeping, and when she looks into the tomb she finally sees the angelic visitors—who have waited until Peter and the beloved disciple have gone home! Though they question her, they do not commission her to go and tell the disciples, for in this gospel, that authority rests with Jesus himself. When she turns away, she sees Jesus, but does not recognize him. Different explanations for this have been attempted: Jesus, raised from the dead, looks different than he did before the resurrection; her eyes were too full of tears, and so on. I think the most likely explanation is that it illustrates the truth of Jesus' words just before the story of the raising of Lazarus: "He calls his own sheep by name and leads them out. When he has brought out all his own, he goes ahead of them, and the sheep follow him because they know his voice" (Jn. 10:3b–4). Just as Jesus called Lazarus by name, summoning him back to life and out of the tomb, so here following his own triumph over the grave Jesus calls to Mary by name and it is in the sound of her name spoken in his voice that she knows him.

Mary then turns and calls out to Jesus in joyful recognition, and the text implies that she either embraces or tries to embrace him. One of the most popular subjects for religious painting historically has been the *Noli Me Tangere* (Do not touch me) in which Mary Magdalene has been depicted reaching out for Jesus, who is fending her off. The NRSV translates Jesus' words not as "do not touch me" but "do not hold on to me." Some writers have seen that as suggesting she *has* embraced him. This is significant because of the prohibition of women touching men who were not their immediate relatives. Though a disciple might be expected to wash the feet of his brethren (exclusive language intentional!) it was radical for a woman disciple to do so. How much more radical, then, for a woman to embrace Jesus? This has been used to defend the currently popular notion that Mary Magdalene was the same woman as Mary of Bethany, and that she was married to Jesus. While unthinkable that a woman should touch Jesus, be in his presence with her hair uncovered, and then feel free to embrace him, it becomes somehow explicable if she was his wife. However romantic the idea, I find it less than compelling, as it is almost as unlikely, excluding the embrace in the garden, that a respectable married woman would do any of those things in public. Of course, if we conflate Mary of Magdala and Mary of Bethany with the sinful woman of Luke's gospel, then I suppose we assume she was not a respectable married woman, or, at least, that that state is relatively new to her.

I find all that supposition, based on what is now generally recognized to have been a mistaken identification, to be far more complicated than it is worth. While in my own view a married Jesus would be no less the Savior, the gospel of John presents women as functioning as an important part of Jesus' life outside the roles acceptable for women in their society. John is, as I have said, a gospel of relationship, and I maintain that *discipleship* is the relationship pointed to by these acts by women. True discipleship among the women is a far more liberating and empowering truth than that Mary Magdalene was privileged because, as John Dominic Crossan said to me in an interview, "she was Mrs. Jesus."[3]

This idea that Mary Magdalene was the wife of Jesus is not a new one. As with all saints, there are many legends about Mary Magdalene. In 1982 Michael Baigent, Richard Leigh, and Henry Lincoln published *The Holy Blood and the Holy Grail,* republished in 1983 as *Holy Blood, Holy Grail.* Reading this book, Margaret Starbird was moved to research and later to believe the French legends about Mary Magdalene retold in *Holy Blood, Holy Grail.* Briefly the legend conflates Mary Magdalene with Mary of Bethany and suggests that this woman was Jesus' wife. Pregnant at the time of the crucifixion, she was taken away from Jerusalem to protect her and her unborn child, a daughter who was born in Egypt. A few years later, Mary and her daughter went to France, where the child, Sarah, became one of the ancestors of the Merovingian kings. *Holy Blood, Holy Grail,* and Starbird's book *The Woman with the Alabaster Jar* see in this story that *Mary* was the holy grail, because she was the vessel that carried the holy blood of Jesus in her womb. This theory does not, on the face of it, make much sense scripturally, not only because such a relationship is never mentioned, but also because, although the disciples were afraid following the crucifixion of Jesus, they were apparently not persecuted immediately by Rome or the Sanhedrin. A wife, even a pregnant one, would have posed no threat to the power structures of the day if Jesus were merely a carpenter or an itinerant preacher. However, Starbird (and, subsequently, Dan Brown in his novel *The Da Vinci Code*) argues that Jesus was much more than a peasant. Jesus was, she argues, descended from King David. If Mary Magdalene were in fact Mary of Bethany, a daughter of the tribe of Benjamin, then the marriage between Jesus and Mary was a dynastic one. Jesus is seen as the rightful heir to the throne of Israel, and his child therefore a distinct political threat.

I must say at this point that my objection to this ingenious theory[4] is based not on legendary material but the scriptures themselves. To be sure, the genealogies of Matthew and Luke present Jesus as descended from David, but Mark is unconcerned with Jesus' ancestors. His identity as the Christ, and what kind of Christ, is what occupies Mark's gospel, as is the case with all the other gospels. They tell us that Jesus himself spoke of a different kingdom and a radically different kind of kingship than that of an earthly king, no matter what his lineage. Although in the Old Testament "messiah" was used as an appellation of king, so was "son of God." Although the people want to believe that in Jesus *messiah* means earthly king, he repeatedly denies this. John reports Jesus does not reply to Pilate's question of whether he is the king of Israel with the short, evasive answer of the synoptics: "You say that I am" (Jn. 18:37). Rather, he repudiates that the title "king of Israel" describes him: "My kingdom is not from this world. If my kingdom were from this world, my followers would be fighting to keep me from being handed over to the Jews. But as it is, my kingdom is not from here" (Jn. 18:36).

Following this disclaimer, his response to the same question again is the familiar, "You say that I am a king. For this I was born, and for this I came into the world, to testify to the truth" (Jn. 18:37a). This is a short discussion, though the examples of Jesus denying any earthly kingship are plentiful in the gospels. Although, no doubt, some of his followers believed or hoped he would be an earthly king, the argument that Jesus was actually the heir to the throne of Israel and therefore his wife and child constituted a political danger seems to be unfounded except in legend. Jesus indeed is King, but the message of all the gospels is that it is a kingdom in no way limited by real estate.

Dan Brown's amazingly popular *The Da Vinci Code* took the mystery of Mary Magdalene to countless readers. It became the subject of book clubs and sermons, public denunciations and defenses of church history and tradition, and provoked a storm of controversy and questions from individual readers to the highest echelons of the church. But it was the discovery of some much older books that truly holds the power to shake up our thinking about women in the life of Jesus; in the earliest communities of Christians following the resurrection; and as church leaders, teachers, and prophets.

In 1896 a German scholar named Carl Reinhardt purchased an ancient papyrus book from an antiquities dealer in Cairo. Included in the book, called a codex, were four previously unknown Christian texts: the *Gospel of Mary,* the *Apocryphon of John,* the *Sophia of Jesus Christ,* and the *Acts of Peter.* These books were written in Coptic, dated from the fifth century C.E., and are now known as the Berlin Codex. In 1917 a tiny fragment of the *Gospel of Mary* was discovered, also in Egypt. Although only a small piece of the *Gospel,* it was written in Greek, and dated to the third century C.E.[5] It presents a startling picture of Mary Magdalene as a powerful leader in the early Christian community. In 1945 a cache of books representing the remains of a Coptic library was discovered near Nag Hammadi in Upper Egypt. Although this amazing find did not include a copy of the *Gospel of Mary*, it did include some of the other books found in the Berlin Codex. Among these were the *Gospel of Thomas,* the *Gospel of Philip,* and the *Sophia of Jesus Christ.* Another small piece of the *Gospel of Mary* was found, however, at Oxyrhynchus in Lower Egypt, also in Greek and dating to early in the third century. In all these writings, Mary Magdalene is presented as a favored disciple and a leader in the Christian movement. In the *Sophia of Jesus Christ,* Mary is one of those gathered to listen to Jesus after the resurrection. Jesus commissions seven women, including Mary Magdalene, along with the twelve male disciples, to go out and preach the gospel. The *Gospel of Philip* tells us that Jesus loved her more than the other disciples and that Jesus used to kiss her often. This last has also added to the assertion by some writers that Jesus had an intimate and perhaps married relationship with Mary Magdalene. The *Gospel of Mary,* however, describes Mary as kissing the disciples, comforting them in their grief over Jesus' departure.[6] This suggests a kiss of peace, or a general sign of affection such as was common among Christians (of either gender) without suggesting any sexual connotation. Therefore the kisses Mary received from the Savior described in the *Gospel of Philip* were more likely of this same type.

These ancient texts do not describe an unequivocally egalitarian society modeled by these early Christians. These writings show dissention over the issue of women's leadership, and a power struggle between Peter and Mary Magdalene. Yet it is undeniable that these books were written in communities where women were not yet precluded from discipleship, or from being teachers and preachers. They also suggest a strong tradition of Mary Magdalene as a powerful leader in the early church, at least in some of the Christian communities. But the seeds of her displacement are already to be seen in these manuscripts, as jealousy of her place and influence is already evident among the other disciples, particularly Peter.

As we consider all the textual material we have (so far) on Mary Magdalene, I think we may discern several things, and must continue to wonder about others, at least until another cache of documents may be found to enlighten, frighten, and challenge us. Mary Magdalene was a follower of Jesus from early in his ministry. She, along with several other women followers, was a woman of property, able to provide financial support to Jesus and his ministry. Mary was an integral part of the passion and resurrection stories in the early church described by all four of the canonical gospels. From the gospels and writings discovered in Egypt, we also now can see that Mary was a disciple and an apostle. There was a strong tradition in the early church, suggested by Mary's prominence in the resurrection stories, as well as descriptions in the Gnostic writings, that there was a deep bond of affection between her and the Savior, and that he held her in high regard. (It has been suggested by some scholars that Mary Magdalene may have been the beloved disciple of John's gospel.[7])

John's gospel makes no mention of Mary Magdalene as having been healed by Jesus of a mental or physical illness, nor does Matthew. The mention of it in Mark's longer ending (added later to the text) and in Luke suggests it may have been added somewhat awkwardly to the texts. Certainly there is no mention of this affliction or healing in the Gnostic texts that describe her as a leader of the church. While Mary's "seven devils" is still part of our tradition about Mary Magdalene, it may in fact not be true at all, but instead reflects a move to discredit her. However, it is still clear that she was integral to the story of Jesus' triumph over death, the principal witness preferred above Peter, John, James, or even the "beloved disciple." Regardless of possible later attempts to minimize or discredit her, Mary Magdalene was so compelling a witness to the resurrection that none of the gospel writers could tell the story without her.

REFLECTION: Rabboni!

They march across the pages, the men and women of the Bible, and their stories inform us of so much—challenge us to think, to imagine, to work, and to dream. They send to us across the eons the stories of God and of man and woman, encountering one another in wildernesses, in cities and in fields of thorn and grain, on the breast of the sea and the bosom of family. They come down to us through centuries of writing, passed down through all the generations, and beyond these the countless centuries and even millennia of oral tradition. These stories speak of a searching God and a searching people, searching for meaning and understanding, and, above all, for relationship. To touch and to be touched by the Divine that is at the heart of all creation, the Beloved who waits for us in every clamorous crowd and every quiet solitary moment—that is the quest that sends us through the pages of the ancient texts. We look for God. And God does not wait for us to find the divine self; God also reaches out to find us, to be revealed in us. This book that we call the Bible is so many things. It contains liturgy and song, history, legend, myth, biography, law and code. But most of all, and most important of all, it is the place where we encounter story.

I remember when I was little, my mother told or read me stories every night of my life. Even when she had all her teeth pulled, and was in severe pain, she managed to sit with me and read. And when my too-fertile imagination was at work in the everyday world, and I was relating some explanation or description of events of grave import, I remember aunts and grandmothers fixing me with skeptical eyes and asking me: "Judy Kaye Pierce—is this a *story?*" And so, at a very early age, I came to comprehend something that shaped my understanding for almost my entire life—there was a difference between truth and story. It was a tragic mistake.

The Christian world could benefit from exploring the Jewish concept of midrash, a way of study and the creation of tools to explain, to explore, and to experience the sacred texts. Midrash is both a method and a product. To study a text with the goal of experiencing it, examining it, finding our way around in it, and especially to listen for echoes of other stories behind it—this is midrash. The stories and art that are created from that experience, art that illuminates the text—that also is midrash. It is a profound adventure. We learn to stop asking the question, "Is it true?" and start asking the question, "What does it mean?"

In studying the accounts of women in the gospel of John, and to some degree the other gospels, we learn something else powerful and haunting. There have been rich, propertied women, and poor beggar women, women guilty of sinful lives, and women elevated to semi-divine as the very epitome of purity and sinlessness. There have been women of Israel and Gentile women, women of wit and wisdom, and women of silent suffering. But one thing is most painfully obvious. Most, not all but most, are nameless. Their names, if they *were* known—and surely, somebody must have known their names as they crowded around Jesus, touching him and being touched by him, living with him, caring for him, in relationship with him—are lost to us now. With the exception of a few—Mary and Martha of Bethany, Mary the mother of Jesus, Joanna and Salome, Mary the mother of James, and of course Mary Magdalene—most of the women pass through the stories nameless. They are remembered because of their stories, because of their relationships with Jesus. Many of the stories are powerful and wonderful and fill us with hope. Yet the fact that their names have been forgotten is both a sad testimony and a warning signal. At a recent workshop on this material, one woman looked thoughtful and, yes, bereaved. "Where did they all go?" she wondered sadly. "The women—there were so many of them, where did they all go?" In some ways, in spite of the vividness of the stories of women in the New Testament, and in the Old as well, we can learn something equally important by the silence that surrounds them. It is what has been left out, or perhaps erased or edited, that touches our hearts and imaginations as we move through the stories of the women in Jesus' life. Who were they? What were their names? What happened to them? The pages are almost silent, for there has been a real, a very real, attempt to forget them.

Think about the stories you know about women in the life of Jesus. There was his mother, remember, amazed by angels and adamant at the wedding of Cana, demanding her miracle of new wine (Jn. 2.1–12). There was the Canaanite woman, the Gentile who dared to infiltrate the all-Jewish band and cry out for healing for her daughter, and in the face of the stinging rebuff from Jesus finds wit and humor to stand up and keep demanding healing and wholeness, and who taught the Savior something about inclusion and justice (Mt. 15:21–28). There was the woman at the well who engaged in a clever and thoughtful discussion with Jesus about ecumenism and received the gift of living water (Jn. 4:4–42), and the woman taken in adultery who was treated by Jesus with respect and kindness and compassion (Jn. 8:2–11). There was the widow who pursued the unjust judge and insisted upon his doing his job and doing it right (Lk. 18:1–8), and the woman who diligently searched her house for a coin and was used as a metaphor for God (Lk. 15:8–10), and the poor widow whose gift of all she had was hailed by Jesus as personifying justification and salvation (Mk. 12:41–44). And, perhaps most poignant of all, there is the woman with the flow of blood who suffered untold degradation, loneliness, and untouchability for twelve years, whose desperation and courage drove her to reach out to seize the hem of Jesus' robe in her search for healing, and whose faith, she was told, had made her whole (Mk. 5:25–34). Everywhere among the clamorous crowds of the rich, powerful, learned, and chosen; everywhere in the press of people destined to be disciples, constantly squabbling, arguing, missing the point and denying the point; everywhere is the witness of the women, reaching out, believing, having faith, holding out for justice, healing, and wholeness. Where are their names? They have been forgotten.

Then there are the named women, such as Junia (Rom. 16:7) whom Paul addresses as a bishop in the early church and whose name was changed by translators of the Bible into Junius, the male form, because it was just unthinkable that a woman could have been a bishop and so, they reasoned, it must have been a typo. And there were Dorcas (Acts 9:36) and Priscilla (Acts 18:2), leaders of the early church commended by Paul, and Joanna and Susanna (Lk. 8:3), women who provided for Jesus "out of their resources.". When did you read about them, or hear about them? Their names are recorded and their stories at least referenced, but there is silence around them in the vast majority of Christian churches in the world. The Roman Catholic Church denies women ordination because, it argues, Jesus didn't ordain any women. Also, it argues that because of Peter's great confession of faith Jesus gave *him* the "keys to the kingdom" and declared *him* the rock upon which the church would be built. Well, so it is recorded in the synoptic gospels, but in the gospel of John the Samaritan woman at the well receives the gift of Christ's revelation of his identity (Jn. 4:26), and it is not Peter but Martha who makes the great confession of faith: "Yes, Lord, I believe that you are the Messiah, the Son of God" (Jn. 11:27).

Another woman from the workshop said she led a study on inclusive language. One of the men of her church, an elder, just couldn't understand what women were "on about." He just couldn't understand why women couldn't get it that masculine language is meant to include everyone. At the end of the study there was a worship service in which they used only feminine language—in the prayers, in the sermon, in the liturgy, and in all the hymns—feminine names for God, female references—only stories about women. The elder said in plaintive tones: "I really feel left out." "Good," she replied, "now you get it."

No thoughtful feminist theologian or preacher of my acquaintance wants to substitute feminine language for masculine. None want to give up the metaphors for God that are masculine—"Father," for example, is a powerful and comforting image for many people, and Jesus clearly loved his earthly father Joseph very much, because surely it is from him that Jesus learned about fathers who love, forgive, and give good gifts to their children. But Jesus had a mother too, a strong woman who had children, who cooked and cleaned, was generous of heart, wanted her children to be safe and to fulfill their promise—a mother who had faith in her son and stayed with him even unto death and beyond. That is the Mary I love and want to remember, not the passive and accepting ever-virgin.

There are too many of us whose names have been erased. Men and women alike, whose stories are cut short or told only in part. And the church has been as bad an offender as any political system in keeping women and minorities under oppression.

I know Jesus went to the cross remembering the names of those who followed him, believed in him, who had comforted him. Men and women, Jew and Greek, slave and free—all named, known, and loved by Jesus, who forgave humanity with his dying breath and who summons us to the table every week with the words "remember me."

Then there is Mary Magdalene. One of the things the early church seems to have done was to have combined the person of Mary Magdalene, faithful follower of Jesus, who supported him out of her means, who is the single person recorded by all four gospels as being present at the cross and at the tomb, with stories of nameless women, particularly the sinful woman in Luke who anointed Jesus' feet and cried a bucket of tears because she was so remorseful for being so terrible a person, so vile, so very, very bad. And Mary Magdalene was also combined, in this early church persona, with the woman taken in adultery, because if she was a sinner, well, there's no sin like adultery; here one is, so let's assume it is she. And then, a real stretch, she was even combined in some old records with the woman at the well. Now why, you may ask? If there is one thing we know about Mary Magdalene actually from the text, it is that she was from Galilee and followed Jesus during his ministry there. The woman at the well, if we know one thing about her, it is that she was a Samaritan, living in Samaria. Her nationality, along with her gender, is crucial to the story. So now how did a Galilean girl like Mary of Magdala get confused with a woman of Samaria? Well, it was simple, really. The woman at the well is guilty of more than being a Samaritan. She has had five husbands, and is now living with a man who is not her husband. She is an immoral woman, living an irregular life. Mary of Magdala, having been confused with a sinful woman, an adulterous woman, has been branded a prostitute—so a woman with too many husbands and a man who isn't her husband—well, it was too good an opportunity to pass up. It is as if some early editor thought, "well there are entirely too many women running around in Jesus life, let's just combine them into one. Here is another immoral, imperfect, unworthy woman just waiting to be subsumed into the legend of Mary Magdalene—the repentant whore of church legend." And she fulfilled a pretty important role in the early church and down through the ages. She is the symbol of repentance. In her, we find hope. After all, if Jesus could forgive her, he could forgive anybody. There's hope for you and me. So let's get it straight, once and for all. Mary Magdalene wasn't a prostitute. She wasn't the sinful woman who cried all over Jesus' feet. She wasn't the woman taken in adultery. And she certainly wasn't the woman at the well. That woman, like all the others, is entitled to her own story.

We know only a few things about Mary of Magdala, things we may derive from the accounts of her in the scriptures. We know that she became one of Jesus' followers, and that she helped financially to support his ministry. We know she followed faithfully even to the foot of the cross. And we know that she followed Jesus even to the tomb, early on Easter morning. There, crouched by the entrance of an inexplicably empty tomb, she followed him into history as the first to witness the risen Christ, and the first evangelist to carry the good news into the future. In the account of Mary Magdalene in the garden we have the perfect paradigm for a life of faith. She went to find Jesus. Finding him, she listened. Listening, she believed. Believing, she went to proclaim the gospel, the good news.

Why did Jesus choose Mary Magdalene to be his messenger? The disciples, good old Peter and the others, were there too, almost as early, available for Jesus to reveal himself. No need to invoke a "middle-woman" in the person of Mary Magdalene. Yet it is to Mary that Jesus appears. He calls her by name. He opens her eyes to the amazing, glorious vision of eternal life. She responds with her own naming—"Rabboni," she cries, "Teacher," recognition and joyful submission all in that one word of response. He entrusts her to take the truth and tell it to the others. He sends her out armed with the good news.

Like all the other gospels, the gospel of John was written to comfort, to exhort, and to teach a specific community of believers. What was so unique about this community that it warranted a gospel with a feminine backbone? We may never know the answer, but at least we can ask the question. One thing is certain. No one may assume that because they are not the obvious person for the job—not the brightest, the fastest, the strongest, the bravest, the most powerful—that they are not going to be entrusted with the message. No one may assume that others will carry the truth to the world, others better suited or more willing. No one may assume that Jesus chooses his standard-bearers using any criteria that we understand. We just never know when he will choose someone to spread the good news to a crying world. It may be you.

Notes

[1] *The Penitent Magdalene,* c. 1453–55. Wood with polychrome and gold. Height 188 cm. Museo dell' Opera del Duomo, Florence.

[2] "She whom Luke calls the sinful woman, whom John calls Mary, we believe to be the Mary from whom seven devils were ejected according to Mark. And what did these seven devils signify, if not all the vices... It is clear, brothers, that the woman previously used the unguent to perfume her flesh in forbidden acts. What she therefore displayed more scandalously, she was now offering to God in a more praiseworthy manner. She had coveted with earthly eyes, but now through penitence these are consumed with tears. She displayed her hair to set off her face, but now her hair dries her tears. She had spoken proud things with her mouth, but in kissing the Lord's feet, she now planted her mouth on the Redeemer's feet. For every delight, therefore, she had had in herself, she now immolated herself. She turned the mass of her crimes to virtues, in order to serve God entirely in penance, for as much as she had wrongly held God in contempt."

Gregory the Great, Homily XXXIII, PL LXXVI, col. 1239 quoted by Susan Haskins in *Mary Magdalen: Myth and Metaphor* (New York: Riverhead Books, 1993).

[3] John Dominic Crossan, interview with the author, 2004.

[4] For more about the grail legend, and Mary Magdalene in the context of the French legends, refer to Margaret Starbird's *The Woman with the Alabaster Jar* (Rochester, Vt.: Bear and Company, 1993) and Michael Baigent, Richard Leigh, and Henry Lincoln's *Holy Blood, Holy Grail* (New York: Dell, 1983).

[5] Of this discovery, Karen King writes: "Yet these scant pages provide an intriguing glimpse into a kind of Christianity lost for almost fifteen hundred years. This astonishingly brief narrative presents a radical interpretation of Jesus' teachings as a path to inner spiritual knowledge; it rejects his suffering and death as the path to eternal life; it exposes the erroneous view that Mary of Magdala was a prostitute for what it is—a piece of theological fiction; it presents the most straightforward and convincing argument in any early Christian writing for the legitimacy of women's leadership; it offers a sharp critique of illegitimate power and a utopian vision of spiritual perfection; it challenges our rather romantic views about the harmony and unanimity of the first Christians; and it asks us to rethink the basis for church authority. All written in the name of a woman." Karen L. King, *The Gospel of Mary of Magdala: Jesus and the First Woman Apostle* (Santa Rosa, Calif.: Polebridge Press, 2003).

[6] Ibid., 14 [Then Mary stood up and greeted] them; she tenderly kissed [them all and said, "Brothers and sisters, do not weep, do not be dis]tressed nor be in doubt." Papyrus Oxyrhynchus, 14–15.

[7] For more on this theory, see Esther De Boer, *Mary Magdalene: Beyond the Myth,* trans. John Bowden (Harrisburg: Trinity Press International, 1997).

Conclusion

I have lived with the women in the gospel of John for thirty years. I have explored their stories in many ways, using many sources. What was an unthinkably radical idea thirty years ago—could the author of John's gospel have been a woman?—is no longer unthinkable. Women scholars of the highest quality today are asking—and answering—that question. The discovery and publication of the Gnostic gospels and other records of early Christian thought previously unknown have shown us an unimagined diversity in the early church. The very structure of the gospel suggests something is going on, something mysterious and evocative. *Why*, after all, in a male-dominated world, and indeed church, would the gospel lift up all these major events and themes built around women? Why choose women to be the paradigms for disciple and evangelist? Could a woman have written the gospel of John? Yes. Could that woman have been Mary Magdalene? Perhaps, or some other woman who had known her and followed her teachings. It is generally accepted that none of the canonical gospels were likely to have been written by any of the close circle of Jesus' disciples. Rather, they were written by followers of those disciples addressing specific church communities that had grown up around their ministries. The gospel of John was probably written not by Mary herself, but by a member of the community known today as "the Community of the Beloved Disciple"—a community in which the ministry and witness of Mary Magdalene were remembered and revered. Could the true authorship have been restructured and disguised to make the gospel more acceptable to the church authorities, who would decide whether or not it was deserving of being included in approved writings, and eventually what we call the canon? Nothing could be more likely, if a woman indeed wrote this gospel. Can we prove it to the established church? Probably not—until that next cache of church writings and records turns up. Perhaps then.

APPENDIX A

Seven-Week Study Guide

Create a sense of visual witness. You may want to create a small worship setting for this Bible study. Something simple, such as using seven candles—one to be lighted each week for each of the women witnesses— can be very effective.

Engage the text. In reading the scripture for each week, I have found the *lectio divina* style of Bible study to be very helpful. Have one person read slowly through the text, and everyone simply listen. Have a second person read it again. This time, participants should note down any word or phrase that particularly captures their attention, or about which they have questions. After the text is read, invite people to share what they heard.

This study assumes that the participants have read the chapter and reflection for the week. If this is not the pattern you wish to follow, the leader could read parts of it aloud, particularly with reference to the main points as given in the outline.

Overall Outline

Week One

John 2:1–12 The Mother of Jesus at Cana
- Mary in the synoptics
    * Birth narratives—ever virgin, perfectly submissive
    * A confused and fearful Jewish mother
- The mother of God, queen of heaven
- Initiates the ministry: new wine, new covenant
    * The perfect disciple

Week Two

John 4:4–42 The Samaritan Woman
- A woman oppressed
    * An unnecessary journey and an unlikely convert
- The Messiah revealed
- New worship
- An eager evangelist and a powerful preacher

Week Three

John 8:2–11 The Woman Taken in Adultery
- An orphan tale–why it belongs
- The mysterious writing
  - * Judgment by ordeal–Old Testament reflection from the book of Numbers
- A new law–amazing grace

Week Four

John 11:1–27 Martha of Bethany
- Martha (and Mary) in Luke
  - * A woman of property
  - * An intimate friendship
- Martha in the gospel of John: character runs true
  - * Activist, worker, caretaker
- The Great Confession and the promise of new life

Week Five

John 12:1–8 Mary of Bethany
- A confusion of Marys
  - * The sinful woman of Luke's gospel
- Mary of Bethany
  - * An intimate relationship
  - * Example of stewardship
- Model of servanthood

Week Six

John 19:25b–27 The Mother of Jesus at the Cross
- The beginning and the end
- The symbols of Cana transformed
- The birth of the church

Week Seven

John 20:1–18 Mary Magdalene
- In the synoptic gospels
- A woman possessed–or powerful?
- A woman of substance and influence
- An undeniable presence
- The great penitent and the triumph of politics
- Mary Magdalene and the early church
- A new cult of Mary–the divine feminine revisited in modern fiction
  - * Called to believe, sent to proclaim

Week One: The Mother of Jesus at Cana

John 2:1–12

Welcome

Light a candle for Mary, Mother of Jesus.

Opening Prayer: God of all beginnings and endings, open our hearts and minds to receive your Word. Send us the spirit of truth that we may learn from the witnesses of the past. Embolden us to ask questions and suggest new answers. Fill us with the wine of your love as we engage the text. Comfort us in the knowledge that only you know the whole story. Amen.

Presentation of main themes

Questions for Reflection

1. What was your understanding of Mary, the mother of Jesus, as you were growing up?
2. (*For the women in the group*) Did Mary provide you a role model? Why or why not?
3. (*For the men in the group*) Did the stories about Mary suggest to you how women should live and act?
4. Which Mary do you identify with the most: the Mary of the nativity, totally obedient to God's will; the Mary who searches for her lost son in the temple; the Mary who tries to get Jesus to stop preaching when it becomes dangerous; the Mary at Cana who bade her son, "Get on with the job"?
5. Have you found a new appreciation of the mother of Jesus that enables you to see yourself in her story?

Closing Prayer: God of all beginnings and endings, help us to encounter you in the events of our lives. Help us to treasure the miracle of your love in the humdrum of everyday, and in the joy of spectacular new beginnings. Help us never to settle for the stale water of the past, but to always clamor for new wine. Amen.

Week Two: The Samaritan Woman

John 4:4–42

Welcome

Light a candle for the Woman of Samaria.

Opening Prayer: God of mountains and deserts, cities and wildernesses, bless us as we set out on new journeys in uncharted territory. Give us courage to see in the stranger's face the glory of your creation. Fill us with the living water, your Son Jesus, that we may never know thirst. Help us to discern in each new encounter an opportunity to share what we have found: a well that never will run dry. Amen.

Presentation of main themes

Questions for Reflection

1. Have you ever been aided or befriended by a stranger while traveling away from home? Have you every befriended someone else in similar circumstances? Did the encounter leave you with any new understanding of your spiritual journey?

2. Who are "those people" in your community (the ones looked down on, viewed with suspicion, the ones we are uncomfortable being around)? Have *you* ever felt like an outsider?

3. Have you ever felt you were without voice or influence in an important area of your life (family, work, church)?

4. Do you feel that you do not have the power or the knowledge to share the good news with others?

5. What about the story of the Samaritan woman might help you to embrace your own power and find your own voice?

Closing Prayer: God of deep shadows and blinding light, allow us to see the Christ in everyone. Encourage us to have a welcome table where no one is an outsider. Help us to throw down the things that hold us back and keep us from freely embracing the Jesus life. Help us to drink deeply from the living water of the promise. Enable us to proclaim the good news with power and joy. Amen.

Week Three: The Woman Taken in Adultery

John 8:2–11

Welcome

Light a candle for the adulterous woman.

Opening Prayer: Forgiving and loving God, we acknowledge the many times we have been unfaithful in our lives: to one another, to ourselves, and to you. With deep humility we ask you to deliver us from being judgmental and fill us with your divine forgiving spirit. Amen.

Presentation of main themes

Questions for Reflection

1. Can you think of a time when you were publicly embarrassed (at school, work, church, playground)? Can you recall how you felt? Was someone kind to you?

2. Does the story of the adulterous woman remind you of any modern-day examples of women being victimized by unjust laws or attitudes, or the unequal application of law?

3. Has your church ever been challenged by having a person in fellowship who was guilty of a crime or of questionable behavior? How did the church express the forgiveness of Christ?

4. What does the story of the adulterous woman say to us about the nature of God's forgiveness of sin?
5. The adulterous woman does not ask for forgiveness, but Jesus gives it to her anyway. What does this story tell us about how we might accept forgiveness, as well as offer it?

Closing Prayer: God of grace and compassion, we give you thanks that, when you look at us, you see not the sum of our sins but the tally of our potential. Free us from the guilt of the past over things done and undone. Help us to open our hearts and accept your forgiveness. Then help us to have forgiving hearts and to offer those who have wronged us not judgment but grace. Amen.

Week Four: Martha of Bethany

John 11:1–27

Welcome

Light a candle for Martha.

Opening Prayer: We find you, O God of all living, in the busyness of our lives. We find you in the quiet moments of our solitary meditations. We find you in joy and sorrow, in life and death, and in desperation and hope. You have given us questioning minds and hearts, and we rejoice to know you want us to use them! Help us to work with glad hearts, but to know when to stop. We know we can call out to you at any time, day or night. Help us to preserve time in our lives to sit at your feet and listen. Amen.

Presentation of main themes

Questions for Reflection
1. An old and popular question—are you a Mary or a Martha, as described in Luke's story? Does the story of Martha and Mary in John 11 change your identification, or strengthen it?
2. What gift or blessing has come to you as a result of being the hard worker or the contemplative? How have you shared it with your church?
3. What do you need to do to embrace the identity you did not choose? Set aside more time for study so you can be more like Mary? Take on a new task with all your energy so you can be more like Martha?
4. Although they have very different personalities and gifts, how are they alike? Considering all the stories, including the anointing in John 12, what do you discern about the sisters' relationship with each other?
5. Have you ever allowed something to be a roadblock to your faith—an event or circumstance that closed off your creativity and openness? How did the stone get rolled away?

Closing Prayer: God of miracles, open our ears to the voice of your Son, who calls us out—out to mission, out to ministry, out to faith. Teach us to nurture our faith in study and in prayer so that even the shadow of the tomb cannot overcome it. Give us voice to proclaim the good news that Jesus is the Christ, your Son, the one who has come into the world who helps us each roll away the stones.

Week Five: Mary of Bethany
John 12:1–8
Welcome
Light a candle for Mary of Bethany.

Opening Prayer: Summon us, O God of infinite patience, away from our selfish concerns and ingrown vision! Summon us to kneel at the feet of your son Jesus, and there to reveal ourselves in all our imperfections, failings, and faults. Help us to strip away the veils of pride and self-importance we hide behind, so that we might kneel to humbly and tenderly anoint the feet of the Savior. May the fragrance of our faith be bountiful and extravagant, and may it be sweet and pleasing to you. Amen.

Presentation of main themes
Questions for Reflection
1. If we are called as faithful Christians to kneel and anoint the feet of Jesus, how do we do that in our everyday world? How does the church do it?
2. Can you think of a time when someone performed a difficult or especially generous task for you, or when you did so for someone else? How did you feel? How do you think Jesus felt?
3. Has a generous gesture or gift of yours ever been misinterpreted or unappreciated? How did it affect you?
4. Is the extravagance of Mary's gift troubling to you? What does it really say about stewardship and outreach?

Closing Prayer: Beloved, give us the grace to see you in every living face. Embolden us to reach out loving hands to soothe and comfort the suffering ones you put in our way. Cleanse us of all fear and hindrance that holds us back from being instruments of healing love in your world. Help us to be aware that, in every act of compassion and tenderness toward anyone in need, we have done it unto you. Amen.

Week Six: The Mother of Jesus at the Cross
John 19:25b–27
Welcome
Light a candle for the Mother of Jesus.

Opening Prayer: Mother and Father God, sometimes life is too hard for us, too hard to think, too hard to breathe, and too hard to believe. We thank you, beloved parent, that when those times are upon us, and the pain is too great to bear, we can crawl into your lap and rest for a while in your everlasting arms. We know that you are not a God who sits above life, but one that indwells within all life, sharing with us the joy and sorrow that comes with being alive. We need your strength to stand firm, but we know that with you all things are possible, even the cross. Amen.

Presentation of main themes

Questions for Reflection

1. When death takes a loved one, the pain can seem too much to bear. How does a life of faith enable us to endure?
2. The mother of Jesus had to watch her child die before her eyes. Where in our world are women watching their children die—from malnutrition, lack of health care, war or street violence? What do Jesus' words to his mother and the beloved disciple from the cross say to us and to the church about our responsibility to the mothers and children of our world? How well are we doing?
3. Have you known someone who has turned grief into a renewed sense of purpose or mission? How has that person brought a new beginning out of an ending?
4. Is your vision of Mary, the mother of Jesus, different now than when you began this study? Do you identify with her more or less?

Closing Prayer: Out of the depths we cry to thee, O Lord! Forgive us for the callous way we ignore the plight of the dying children of our world. Forgive us for closing our ears to the anguish of their mothers who must see their little ones sacrificed to war or disease. Forgive us for not doing our utmost to demand justice for the little ones in whom reside the hope of the future. Help us, O God, to treasure the children, and to take action on their behalf, for, truly, each one is your precious child. Amen.

Week Seven: Mary Magdalene

John 20:1–18

Welcome

Light a candle for Mary Magdalene.

Opening Prayer: God of the ages, forgive us for all the times we heard your word and dismissed the messenger as unreliable. Forgive us for allowing stereotypes to govern our judgment and determine for us what some people may do and others not. Forgive us for allowing labels to serve in place of knowledge and understanding. Rid us of jealousy and prejudice that we might be found worthy to speak the good news to all who long to hear it.

Presentation of main themes

Questions for Reflection

1. Did you read *The Da Vinci Code* by Dan Brown? Did you watch the movie? Did you find it thrilling? challenging? enlightening? maddening?

2. Have you ever been accused of something you didn't do? Did it diminish your sense of self-worth?
3. Where do you see the damage of "labeling" people (bright, stupid, lazy, immoral, nosy, selfish, proud, etc., etc.) in your world? How do we avoid labeling?
4. Do you feel more empowered by the stories of Mary Magdalene and the other women in John's gospel, or threatened?

Closing Prayer: God of the present, we give you thanks for all those who have told your story! We give you thanks for witnesses to the gospel who heard, believed, and proclaimed that all might know Jesus Christ. Help us to be unafraid in the face of new ideas that challenge our old understanding and way of doing things. Give us the grace to admit to mistakes and do our best to speak the truth fearlessly. Help us, no matter how great our sense of inadequacy, to summon the courage to answer when called, and to go joyfully when sent. Amen.

APPENDIX B

Worship Series

"Driving Away the Dark"

I developed this seven-week series for worship around the study of the women in the gospel of John. Each Sunday focused on one of the women witnesses, using scripture, proclamation, drama, music, and visual art to explore her story. I have done the series twice, with the principal difference between the two times being that in one series we used the dramatic monologues as the message, and the second time we had a homily about each woman and ended the series on Easter morning with a performance of the play "The Women's Tale" (found at the end of this worship section). The play is structured so that communion may be served by the women characters, and hymns or special music inserted at appropriate points. (The monologues were incorporated into the play). In this design I include both options. I have included a description of the art installations that accompanied both series.

In addition to the hymns I mention, I have included an original song at the beginning of the worship section. We used one verse every Sunday, and then sang the entire song on Easter.

Given that orders of service vary from denomination to denomination, and sometimes from church to church, I have included some elements that help illuminate the theme of the seven Sundays of the "Driving Away the Dark" Series. I have included hymns from the *Chalice Hymnal* (Chalice Press) and *The New Century Hymnal* (The Pilgrim Press), as well as a few anthems and songs from other sources. These represent only a small number of the wonderful resources available. It is a case of, yet again, "seek, and ye shall find."

Behold a Woman

Behold a woman at a wedding,
Watching Jesus for a sign,
Sees his sorrow, sees his glory,
Water changing into wine.

(Chorus)
I am the light, you're the light of the world,
I am the vine, you are the branches.
I am the bread, you're the salt of the earth,
I am the way, the truth, the life.

Behold a woman in a desert,
Endless thirst no well can heal,
Jesus gives her living water,
Light and life and world reveal.
    (Chorus)

Behold a woman dragged to judgment,
One in shame where two should stand,
"Woman, where are your accusers?
God's compassion is at hand."
    (Chorus)

Behold a woman run to meet him,
"Had you for me no love to give?"
"Believe that I am your messiah,
Though you should die, yet shall you live."
    (Chorus)

Behold a woman humbly kneeling,
Bathes with love and sweet perfume,
Soothes the soul of the anointed,
Ransom's fragrance fills the room.
    (Chorus)

Behold a woman standing by him,
Blood and water flow like wine,
Sees his sorrow, sees his glory,
World redeemed by love divine.
    (Chorus)

Behold a woman in a garden,
At his word all grief has fled,
"Do not seek here for the living,
I have risen from the dead."
    (Chorus)

Words by Judith Jones

First Sunday in Lent: New Wine

Responsive Call to Worship

O Christ, we search for your signs and your wisdom
  at a wedding and at a well.
O Christ, we listen for your promise of forgiveness and hope
  at a temple and at a grave.
O Christ, we pray for your spirit to triumph
  at the table and at the cross.
O Christ, we witness your triumph rising
  at the tomb and in the garden.
O Christ, we search, listen, pray, and witness to the glory of your
  name.

OR

Come to the wedding.
Come to the well.
Come to the temple.
Come to the vigil.
Come to the table.
Come to the cross.
Come to the garden.
Come in courage, come in faith, come in hope. Come.

Old Testament Reading: Psalm 104:10–15

New Testament Reading: John 2:1–12

Message or Monologue: "New Wine: Mary at Cana"

Anthem: "At a Wedding Feast in Cana,"[1] *Oremus Hymnal,*
by Vincent Uher

Solo: "My Soul Gives Glory to My God" *Chalice Hymnal,* no. 130,[2] *New Century Hymnal,* no. 119

Hymn: "Mary, Woman of the Promise," *New Century Hymnal,* no. 123

New Wine: Mary at Cana

I remember clearly how it all happened. But understanding it—well, that came later. We were invited to the wedding, all my children. Jesus had been in Bethany, and I know he had seen his cousin John. John was there, preaching his heart out to the crowds. He was like that, preaching fire on their heads one minute, quenching it in the Jordan the next. Something happened there, between them. I was anxious when he left. I knew—no, I *felt* that something was changing. But he returned in time to go to Cana for the wedding. I remember looking at him, his face so dear and familiar, I thought I knew every mood, every expression. But somehow his face was withdrawn, remote from me. I worried about it, as we traveled. I didn't ask him about it—in spite of reports to the contrary, I do not nag my children! But I worried.

Well, we got to the wedding, and everyone joined the fun. You know how it is at family celebrations: you eat, you talk, you drink a little wine—all right, a lot of wine. The food, it was fine; the mother of that household is a good cook, but the wine—well, it was not so good. Don't misunderstand; it was not so bad, either. So there we were, eating, talking, drinking wine—and I noticed that most of the pitchers of wine were empty. I wasn't snooping, you understand, but family is family and God forbid everyone should be shamed by the wine running out in the middle of a wedding! I looked at the servants, meaning just to hint that they should fill up the pitchers before anyone noticed. They fell all over themselves telling me that there wasn't any more wine. Well, I couldn't believe it. No wine! And what they had, not so good to start with. How could this have happened? My family would be disgraced, the young couple shamed before their friends. I looked around, and saw my son Jesus standing nearby, talking with his brothers and friends. I have no idea why I mentioned to him that they were running out of wine. They were kin, and I didn't want them to be embarrassed, I suppose. But really, it wasn't his business to fix it. He looked at me, I remember, and the look on his face... It was exactly the way he used to look before going out into the town on some little errand. I've seen it a thousand times. "I know I am big and strong, and I know I must be about my tasks, but...it really is all right, isn't it? Safe? You will be here when I get back?" Never saying any of it, you understand, but his face *speaking* it? He said something, reminding me that it wasn't his business to interfere. Well—for years, he had been the man of the house, you understand, since Joseph died. I just turned to him as I always did. "They have no wine," I said. Just that. "They have no wine." Then he looked at the water jars standing nearby, and I'd seen *that* look before, too. When he'd solved some problem or other, or had decided on just the right way to begin a job of work.

Then—well, he looked at me with eyes that were on fire with something that was not grief or anger or joy or hope or anything else, but rather everything at once, and something more. He stepped back from me, and I could tell he wasn't seeing me, or the empty water jars, or the wedding guests, or anything else that I could see. His eyes—his whole *being*—were fixed on something beyond my sight. He motioned toward the servants.. "Do whatever he tells you," I told them. He had them fill the jars—*huge* jars—with water, and I saw the water as it went splashing in. *(Pour water from clear jar into pitcher.)* I felt my heart shrink inside me. I don't know what I expected—I don't know that I really expected anything. I knew that my son had changed, that my little boy had gone forever, and something wonderful and terrible was going to happen. And I knew that it *had* to happen. The noise of the talking, the dancing—it all faded to silence around me. I could not see anything but those jars of water.

I think my heart stopped.

The servants tipped the jars, and I saw a stream of deep red flowing out, pouring out, spilling out: wine, new wine, wine like blood, rivers of sweet wine. I see it still. *(Pour juice or wine from pitcher into clear chalice on table.)* This wine was not conceived in the belly of a grape.

You need two props for this: a clear glass container of water, and an opaque pitcher, which contains the grape juice or wine. "Mary" pours a small amount of water into the pitcher, and then, at the moment indicated, she pours out the juice into a chalice.

Notes

[1] "At a Wedding Feast in Cana," *Oremus Hymnal,* by Vincent Uher. I found this on the Web, and Rev. Uher most kindly allowed me to use it for the Cana service. It is sung to Geneva 42, which in *Chalice Hymnal* is the tune to "Comfort, Comfort You My People," no. 122, and *New Century Hymnal,* no. 101 (where the same tune is called "Psalm 42"). The choir should sing it at a very quick and lively pace, as befits the gaiety of a wedding. Rev. Uher's Web address: www.oremus.org/hymnal/uher

[2] *Chalice Hymnal,* no.131 is the text of the Magnificat, Luke 1:46b–55, as a responsive reading, with a canticle by Miriam Therese Winter. This can be read responsively by the congregation, and the canticle either sung by the congregation, or by a soloist who would then sing #130. *New Century Hymnal* has "Canticle of Mary" presented in a similar way, with reading and sung response, p. 732.

Second Sunday in Lent: Water That Is Alive

Old Testament Reading: Isaiah 35:1–10

Gospel Reading: John 4:4–42

Message or Monologue: "Living Water: The Woman at the Well"

Anthems

"Living Water," words and music by Miriam Theresa Winter, *Woman Prayer, Woman Song: Resources for Ritual* (Oak Park, Ill.: Meyer Stone Books, 1987)

"Mallaig Springling Song," *Common Ground: A Song Book for All the Churches* no. 82 (Edinburgh: St. Andrew Press, 1998)

Solo

"Mystery," words and music by Miriam Theresa Winger, *Woman Prayer, Woman Song: Resources for Ritual.*

Hymns

"Source and Sovereign, Rock and Cloud," (opening hymn of praise) *Chalice Hymnal,* no. 12

"Fill My Cup, Lord," (communion) *Chalice Hymnal,* no. 351

"With Joy Draw Water," *New Century Hymnal,* no. 109

"When, like the Woman at the Well," *New Century Hymnal,* no. 196

"Come, Thou Fount of Every Blessing," *Chalice Hymnal,* no. 16

Water That Is Alive: The Woman at the Well

He looked tired. That was the first thing I noticed. Tired, and hot, and dusty from the roads. I was looking at him, but I tried not to let him see that I was looking at him. It was the sixth hour, and the sun was cruelly hot. It was always hot when I went to the well for water. I could not go when the other women went, in the morning. I would see them from my doorway, all in a bunch, talking and jabbering and laughing as they went to draw water from Jacob's well. They would draw aside from my door when they passed, and they would not look at me. It was nonsense, what they talked, such foolish nonsense those women talked. I would stand there, in the shadow cast by the door, and listen to them, peek out at them, and my heart would bleed with longing to be with them, to be included in all that foolish talk, to be one of them. Oh, I must have cried enough water to fill a well, for all the good it did me. There was not enough water in the wide world to wash me clean enough for them. Well, so there I was, in the heat of the day, and there he was, and I could see he was a Jew. So I was careful, because even though I was not respectable, I didn't want him to insult me or—or even spit on me. You think sometimes there is nothing else that can shame you, and then—someone thinks of a way.

I drew my shawl around me, and tried to make myself small inside it. I came near the well, and I was reaching down to draw the water when—and I'll never forget it because I nearly died of the shock—he spoke to me. In broad daylight! He asked me for a drink. I looked around to see who he was talking to. I only had the one dipper, and I knew he wouldn't dream of drinking out of it. I said something idiotic; I asked him what was he thinking! Did he propose to put his lips where my unclean, Samaritan lips had rested? I was afraid. My throat was so dry I could hardly force the words past my lips. Then he smiled at me. Have you any idea how long it had been since anyone had smiled at me? And then he said that if I knew who I was talking to, I would have asked *him* for a drink, and that he would give me water that was *alive.*

I stood there, in that cruel hot sun, my throat aching, my eyes dry from too many tears shed, and he talked about water that was alive. "Well," I managed to say, "the well is about a hundred feet deep, and you don't seem to have a dipper. Where is this living water?" Then he answered me. That's all. It may not sound like much, now. He listened to me, and he answered me. We talked together, he and I. About me, my lonely, wasted life—too many men and not one love—and about God. And somehow God didn't feel so remote, up there on his holy mountain, or in Jerusalem, depending on who you're talking to. God seemed—there. I knew, then. I don't know how, but I knew. "I know that Messiah is coming," I told him. I looked into his eyes and he smiled again. "I am," he said. That's all. "I am." And I knew it was the truth—the truth, which poured out around me like a fountain in the desert, like a river, like a never-ending stream. So I put down my jug and I ran back to my village—because, when you have found something so wonderful as water that is alive, well...you want to share it, don't you? And you know, they listened to me, and they went to see and hear him. *They listened to me!* I still have to go to Jacob's well for everyday water. But now I go with the others. And we all talk—silly, nonsense talk—and laugh. Sometimes, we talk about that other water, that spring in what was the desert of our souls, that water that is *alive!*

Third Sunday in Lent: The Sound of Stones Falling

Responsive Old Testament Reading: Psalm 32
Sung Response: *Chalice Hymnal,* no. 739 or "You Are My Hiding
Place," *Chalice Hymnal,* no. 554

Gospel Reading: John 8:2–11

Message or Monologue: "The Sound of Stones Falling: The
Adulteress"

Anthem

"Amazing Grace," by Diana White

> Santa Barbara Music Publishing, P.O. Box 41003
> Santa Barbara, CA 93140

Solos

"Forgiving Eyes," by Michael Card, at www.michaelcard.com

"You Are the Song," by Miriam Theresa Winter, *Woman Prayer, Woman
Song: Resources for Ritual*

Hymns

All Hail the Power of Jesus' Name! (Opening Hymn of Praise) *Chalice
Hymnal,* no. 91

"Over My Head," *New Century Hymnal,* no. 514

"It Is Well with My Soul," *Chalice Hymnal,* no. 561

"Come, You Disconsolate," *Chalice Hymnal,* no. 502

"There's a Wideness in God's Mercy," *Chalice Hymnal,* no. 73

"You Are My Hiding Place," *Chalice Hymnal,* no. 554

"Amazing Grace!" *Chalice Hymnal,* no. 546

The Sound of Stones Falling: The Adulteress

I remember, when I was very little, that I used to collect stones from
the fields near our house. I would build little houses, and lay straw and
twigs across to make a roof. My little stone village even had a well in the
center—a hole I scooped out of the dust, with stones around it, and I would
fill it with water from my mother's big jar in the kitchen. As I worked, I
would sing. I sang as I carried the stones; I sang as I built my village; I sang
as I carried water. I remember the woman who lived next to us shaking

her head as she watched me. I heard her say to my mother, "She lives in a dream world." My mother smiled, and shrugged. "Let her sing and dream, while she may," was all she would say.

Then life changed for me. I was given in marriage, and my husband was not the sort to tolerate dreaming or singing when there was work to be done. I cleaned, cooked, and carried water, and occasionally I helped remove stones from the fields. But there was no music in my work, nor in my life. How can life be full of activity, busy from each moment to the next, yet still be empty? How can there be ceaseless sound–the chatter of voices, the grinding of grain on stone, the snoring of sleepers, the lowing of animals, yet all seem silent? You know what happened. I met a man, and he paid attention to me. He smiled, and he wooed me, and I fell into temptation. Life was empty, without purpose or meaning. What did it matter? I mattered to no one, not even to myself. So I became an adulteress.

My husband must have suspected, for he set watchers, and we were caught. I suppose I did matter to him, when it came to someone else possessing his property. Even after all this time, I can barely bring myself to remember that afternoon. They came crashing into my house, those men, and dragged me out into the street. The shock of them, suddenly there in the room, their rough hands seizing me, forcing me through the door without letting me cover myself, dragging me along the dusty road–it deadened my senses. I remember it seemed dark, though it was mid-day. Voices shouted and howled around me, but I couldn't understand the words. I must have fallen, and been dragged, but at the time I didn't feel the pain. Then they flung me down at the feet of a man seated in the temple, and as I lay there in the dirt, my mind cleared a little. Humiliation greater than the sea flooded me, and I lay there, drowning in it, praying for it to be over soon.

I knew they would kill me. I caught a glimpse of someone stooping for a stone. I wondered, through the sea of shame, how long it would take them to kill me; whether someone would hit me in the head with one of the first stones, killing me quickly, or if it would take all afternoon to die. I heard one of them telling the man, there in temple with everyone listening, and looking at me, that I was an adulteress, and asking him if they should stone me to death. I tried to peek up at him, tried to see the face of this man who would judge whether I lived or died. He bent down, and wrote something in the dust. I tried to see what it was, but I was afraid to lift my head. Then I heard him say, "If you have never sinned, then throw your stone." My flesh shrank on my bones, tried to melt into the dust, cringing away from that first cruel pain of striking stone. I couldn't even cry. And we waited, he and I, for the rain of death to fall on me.

But nothing happened. It got quiet; there was no sound at all, except for the sound of stones falling, just falling out of their hands, and then I heard shuffling steps as if people were…*leaving*. He went on writing in the dust, and this time I did lift my head to look into his face. He was looking at me. And more than that, he was *seeing* me. Not just the lonely wife. Not just the adulterous woman. He was seeing *me:* the builder, the singer, the dreamer. "Where are your accusers?" he asked me. I looked around then, and saw...no one. "Does no one accuse you?" he asked. I shook my head then, and managed to whisper, "No one." He smiled then, in that *seeing* way, and said, "Neither do I accuse you. Go now, and sin no more." I stood up, and looked down at the dust where he had been writing. His quick fingers had erased what had been written there, before I could see. But I know what it was, because he wrote the words on my heart as well as in the dust. He had written forgiveness. He had written mercy. He had written music. He had written my dreams.

Fourth Sunday in Lent: Rolling the Stone Away

Old Testament Reading: Ezekiel 37:11–14

Gospel Reading: John 11:1–27

Message or Monologue: "Rolling the Stone Away: Martha of Bethany"

Anthem

"Once We Sang and Danced with Gladness"
> Susan Briehl, Marty Haugen
> GIA Publications, Inc.
> 7404 S. Madison Ave., Chicago, IL 60638

Hymns

"I Want to Be Ready," *New Century Hymnal,* no. 616

"Jesus the Christ Says," *New Century Hymnal,* no. 48

"Come, You Disconsolate," *Chalice Hymnal,* no. 502

"O Christ, the Healer," *Chalice Hymnal,* no. 503

"Healer of Our Ev'ry Ill," *Chalice Hymnal,* no. 506

"Out of the Depths," *Chalice Hymnal,* no. 510

"Out of the Depths I Call," *New Century Hymnal,* no. 483

"I Must Tell Jesus," *New Century Hymnal,* no. 486

Rolling the Stone Away: Martha at Bethany

You know how it is that you can love someone, and still be so mad at that person you can hardly bear it? It was like that for me, that day when I saw Jesus coming up the road. I thought about how my brother had lain in his sick bed, calling for Jesus. Not because he wanted a miracle, mind you. Lazarus would never think of asking anything for himself. No, he just wanted to see his dear friend one last time. I remember my sister looking at me, across his sick bed, her eyes dark with sorrow, asking, asking…, "Why doesn't he come?" We waited, and our brother grew weaker, and finally he stopped calling, stopped looking toward the window, stopped…breathing. I couldn't believe it! Jesus had not come, had sent no word, nothing. All those others he had healed, comforted, and not one word for us, for his friend Lazarus whom he loved. I had gone out of the house, unable to look at my sister any longer. She just sat there, not moving, not speaking, not crying—frozen with pain, disappointment, and grief. Mary—well, she takes things so to heart, even little things. I've seen her cry her eyes out over a dead bird, or a lamb born too soon, too weak to live. And she was never one to go near people; I couldn't believe my eyes when she started to creep into the room and listen to Jesus when he came. After that, she just lived for those times when Jesus would come, and she could sit at his feet and listen to what he said. Still as a mouse, she would listen as if her life depended upon it. Oh, I can be a little impatient with her; I know it. It's a beautiful thing to see a young person lit up with joy, living in a world of the spirit. But it's one less pair of hands to make the bread and wash the clothes. It's fine to talk about the bread of life, but between us, there had also better be bread on the table when everyone's hungry from all that talking! That's the difference between us. I live in *this* world. I've baked many a loaf of bread for Jesus, and given him room in my house to sleep, and taken care that he knew he was loved! And when my brother needed him, I wanted him to come! I trusted him to come. But he didn't.

Then, when Lazarus was already dead and buried in the tomb , *then* I saw Jesus coming up the road toward my house. I was filled with pure rage! I wanted to shake him, scream at him, and tell him how he had failed us. How he had failed my brother, who only wanted to see him one more time, hear the sound of his voice, or touch his hand. Was it so much to ask, I wondered? So, before I knew it, I was running, running toward him, shaking my fist in the air, and crying. I don't do that often, you know. I'm usually the one everyone runs to when they are in trouble. I'm called on to be strong, to take charge. How many tears have soaked into these shoulders, I wonder, as I soothed and patted and assured someone who was crying out their woes in my arms? Well, this time I didn't feel strong, and I didn't feel calm, and there was no one there to hold or comfort me.

He stopped, and waited for me. Then, in the midst of all that rage and yelling and crying, I stopped, too. He was looking at me, and I knew that he had the power to make everything all right. I don't know how I knew. Miracle stories are fine when they are about someone else. But my brother was dead, dead and buried and gone, and yet here I was, certain that Jesus could somehow make it all right. I didn't even dare to put it into words. All I could say was, "If you had been here, my brother would not have died. And if you ask God for something, anything, God will give it to you." He stood there in the road, with the sun all around him, and the look of pure love shining out of his eyes, and tears, too: tears for my brother, for my sister, for me. And I knew that everything would be all right. And then he asked me if I believed that Lazarus would rise again. Now, the teachers have told us for a long time that the righteous will rise on the last day. And surely my brother was righteous. So I said yes, I knew he would rise on the last day. But that was not what I wanted, and Jesus knew it. I wanted life for my brother, life here and now! I know it was unreasonable; I know it was selfish. But I wanted my brother to live! Then Jesus talked to me, in the way he had talked to others in my house, many times. But this time I was not too busy to listen. I heard his words, and they wrote themselves on my heart in letters of fire that have never gone out. "I am the resurrection and the life. If you believe in me, even if you are dead, you shall live. And everyone who lives and believes in me shall never die."

Now, I'm not saying I understood everything, all at once. We went to the tomb, and when he asked me to roll the stone away, I was confused and frightened. First of all, I could not roll away that great stone. And I was afraid of what lay on the other side. I didn't understand, but somehow...I believed. Mary says that is the greatest part of his teaching. When Jesus speaks to you, it writes words of fire on your heart, and you believe. And believing, you shall never die. So we rolled the stone away and faced death. And you know what happened. Death became life. We didn't know that day, as we saw Lazarus come out of the tomb, that soon, too soon, we would stand at another tomb, and weep. But we should have known that no tomb could hold him, no stone separate him from us. I still live in this world, with my brother and sister. We live, and we shall die. But I know, because the words still burn on my heart, that, when we do at last die, Jesus will be there, rolling the stone away.

Fifth Sunday in Lent: The Fragrance of Faith

Old Testament Reading: Isaiah 43:16-21

Gospel Reading: John 12:1–8

Anthem

"Magdalen[1], Cease from Sobs and Sighs,"[2] *The Oxford Choral Songs,*
Oxford University Press

Message or Monologue: "The Fragrance of Faith: Mary of Bethany"

Hymns

"Woman in the Night," *Chalice Hymnal,* no. 188

"A Woman Came Who Did Not Count the Cost," *New Century Hymnal,*
no. 206

"Savior, An Offering Costly and Sweet," *New Century Hymnal,* no. 536

"I Want to Be Ready," *New Century Hymnal,* no. 616

"Said Judas to Mary," *New Century Hymnal,* no. 210

The Fragrance of Faith: Mary of Bethany

I know others remember the other supper, the last one. But I remember that dinner table in my sister's house, before everything ended, and began again. I remember the smell of the flowering almond tree outside the window, all the world fresh with the smell of evening rain: life coming back to the dead land, the promise of spring, and the unbearable sweetness of life. He sat at the table, and talked. Martha had prepared a special meal, and if you have ever eaten at Martha's table, you know that *that* is special indeed. Everything must be just so, just right. It wasn't the Sabbath, just a meal, but for him, well, every day was a celebration of life. But I saw the end in his face. I remember looking at him and thinking, "Oh God, not yet, not yet!" But his eyes told me everything. He had taught us about letting go of things, of not letting anything possess us—not even your own life. In his eyes I saw that he was letting go of everything he loved, all of us, all except God. I looked around, wondering why none of them spoke about it, why Peter didn't jump up and down and tell him not to think like that, things were just getting going, no time to be talking about the end—but he didn't. He didn't understand. He didn't see. None of them saw. Except me.

I've never been able to do things like other people. I'm not that good a cook. And I have never wanted to marry. People can't understand that. They say that's all daughters are good for—to marry and have children. I used to cry myself to sleep when I thought about leaving home, going to someone else's house, being someone's wife. I couldn't bear it. I know you all think Martha is bossy. Well, she is. But she always understood how it was with me. She used to say, "Never mind, little mouse. You shall stay at home and be my joy." I know I make her impatient sometimes, but she always let me stay at home where I wanted to be. Then Jesus came. And I didn't feel helpless and stupid any more. I understood that it was my part to listen, and to understand.

So I understood that we had come to the end. And I wondered what I could do for him, anything to show how much I loved him and thanked him for loving me. We put sweet spices and herbs on the dead. What do we do to perfume the life of the living? I got the nard we had bought and saved, and I anointed his feet with it, and he smiled at me. Martha understood. The others were angry—such *expense.* Some of them—well, they never understood that we were to have him for just a little while. I had heard about the gifts from the visitors when he was born: frankincense and myrrh. It seemed—well, his life was the fragrance of hope for everyone who knew him—so it just seemed... *right* to give him the sweetness of spring to remember us by. I poured it out and the fragrance filled the room.

Notes

[1] This anthem is one that conflates Mary Magdalene with Mary of Bethany. It is, however, a lovely anthem, so use it as a testament to both women.

[2] *New Century Hymnal* includes a verse about Mary that is not included in *Chalice Hymnal.*

Sixth Sunday in Lent: My Son, My Son

Old Testament Reading: Isaiah 53:2–5

Gospel Reading: John 19:25b–27

Message or Monologue: "My Son, My Son: Mary at Golgotha"

Anthem

"And All the World Was Silent," BSC9816

> Charlotte Lee and Douglas E. Wagner
> Belwin Sacred Choral Services
> Warner Bros. Publications, Warner Music Group
> 15800 N.W. 48th Ave., Miami, FL 33014

Hymn

"Born in the Night, Mary's Child," *New Century Hymnal,* no. 152

"Were You There?" *New Century Hymnal,* no. 229

"Journey to Gethsemane," *New Century Hymnal,* no. 219

My Son, My Son: Mary at Golgotha

They tell me it was dark. I had no vision to spare for the sky. I stood there, not alone, yet more alone than I shall ever be again. Those who also loved him best were there, with me, but I have no memory of their faces or their tears. I have no memory of their loving arms as they sheltered me against the enormity of loss and held me up when bone and muscle would have crumpled and failed. I have no memory of their voices, soft and shaken. Now their voices sing me to sleep, voices of comfort, and of hope. Now their voices speak out boldly, powerfully of the message of the Messiah. They are my sisters and daughters, inheritors of the good news.

But I do not remember them there, in that place. I remember only the face and the voice of my son. And I remember the pain.

I cannot tell you about his death, because even now I do not dare open the floodgates to such memories. Some things are best left to be told by those who were not there, who could not see, could not hear, could not feel. I did not want to go, but I went because I could not stay away. I had labored for his birth. I watched his growth to manhood with the same hopes and pride every mother feels for every beloved child. Yet I always knew that this child, this son would not be like every other. This child understood his own life according to a design I could not always see. But when he spoke to me, his eyes alight, I believed in it as though I could see it. I can only say that when he spoke to me, his words were true. I know it as I know the beat of my own heart. I did not want to be there.

There, in that place, the entire world became pain. I breathed it, I writhed under it, it crushed my heart, and it was all I could do to hold on. But, you see, it might be that my presence there comforted him a little—the way I comforted him when he was little, and hurt or frightened, before the great vision took him and left him so little room for fear—or, rather, made it irrelevant. Nothing could take away the agony he suffered, but just in case my being there, loving him... Well, I *had* to be there.

I have other children. I have sons and daughters who look to me to be strong and continually faithful. They seem to think it important that I be here, still part of the story that continues to unfold. I tell them, "We are at only the very beginning of the journey, you and I." I am not comfortable when some of them want to set me apart, as if I were somehow not quite human. They don't understand that *that* is the most wonderful part of this journey we are on to make God's kingdom real. The vision is vested in us, the real, ordinary people who live, love, and die as people have for thousands of years, and will go on doing until the end. Do not make me out to be more than I am, I say. For what I am is quite enough. I am a woman who had a child. That child was filled up with God in a way the world has never seen and shall never see again. He embodied God. And God summoned me to be one of his disciples, so that all women everywhere would see that the kingdom is theirs, too.

I cannot speak about the day he died. And, you know, my son came among us to teach us all how to live. That is what I remember. And so should you.

Easter Sunday: Rabboni!

Old Testament Reading: Isaiah 65:17-25

Gospel Reading: John 20:1–18

Message or Monologue: "Rabboni! Mary Magdalene in the Garden"

Anthem

"You Shall Be My Witnesses," by Miriam Theresa Winter, *Woman Prayer, Woman Song: Resources for Ritual*

"When Mary Through the Garden Went," no. BSC9841

> Choral Music of Douglas E. Wagner
> Warner Bros. Publications, Warner Music Group
> 15800 N.W. 48th Ave., Miami, FL 33014

Hymns

"Woman, Weeping in the Garden," *Chalice Hymnal,* no. 223

"I Come to the Garden Alone (In the Garden)," *New Century Hymnal,* no. 237; *Chalice Hymnal,* no. 227

"Ruler of Life, We Crown You Now," *New Century Hymnal,* no. 228

"Christ Rose Up from the Dead," *New Century Hymnal,* no. 239

"O Sons and Daughters, Sing Your Praise," *Chalice Hymnal,* no. 220

Rabboni! Mary Magdalene in the Garden

In the beginning...yes, I remember the beginning. So vivid I can't always tell the *then* from the *now.* My life before was so...terrible. Oh, I know what people say of me, but the plain truth is that I had been the victim of a terrible illness. My mind was dark, darker than any desert night, and the demons possessed me. I can remember only enough of what it was like to be unwilling to remember more. The most terrible part was that a tiny corner of my mind remained my own, aware. Oh yes, I was aware of the stares, the whispers, the pity and fear. I was aware of the coming of the demons. Then the darkness would take me, and my body would become a battleground for them, screeching, clamoring for possession. I never knew when it would seize me—in the middle of a meal, or as I walked to the well with the other women, or as I was talking with a friend.

I would be so...ashamed. People were afraid, you know. They whispered that I must be a terrible sinner, to be so afflicted. No man would marry me, of course. No dowry was big enough to overcome my illness. Demons, they called it. People would hurry their children indoors when

I passed—as if I might, you know, hurt them. I don't know how I stood it, all those years. Then, he took it all from me: the demons, the pain, the shame, and the terrible sense of guilt. My tiny mind-self would pray for God to release me in death. Instead, God released me to life. You take so much for granted, you who have never been owned by demons: the smell of morning; the sound of birds singing, chattering; the warmth of the sun; the shining mystery of the moon; the touch of someone's hand, strong and comforting, driving away the dark. He gave me all that. And I stopped wanting anything in the world except to be near him, to help him, to love him. Just to hear the sound of his voice. I was born that day. I'll love him until I die. If only I could have died for him. I only wish we could have had...just a little more time.

So you want to know how it was, that early morning when I went to grieve over the body of my Lord? It was quiet, and the cold and darkness of night lingered among the stones and trees. No bird sang. No small huddled creatures made a sound. I was alone as I had never been, not even in my illness. I had left his mother at last and come alone to the tomb. I thought it might comfort her to know that I had been there, although I couldn't go in and tend to him because of the stone. They had sealed the tomb, you see, because they were afraid someone would steal him away. So I knew I couldn't go in, couldn't even clean his wounds or lay a few flowers on his breast. It was pointless, really, going there, but something drew me and I couldn't resist. I walked up the slope, and I felt as if my body was made of stone. My eyes were dry as dust, dry as death. My heart felt like a stone, filling my chest, crowding out the air, because...*the stone was rolled away.*

I stood there, like a fool, staring without seeing, without understanding. The stone was rolled away. I stooped and looked in, but—even now I cannot make my lips to shape the words. I fell down then, and all I could think was, "They've taken his poor body, broken and dishonored, they've robbed us of even his bones to mourn over." I know that others came then, Peter and John, drawn there as I was, and then they ran off again. But I couldn't move, couldn't make sense of anything. It was as if the darkness possessed me again, as if the demons had returned. Finally, I stood up and turned to go. And there was this man standing there. My eyes, dry for so many hours, were suddenly filled with tears, hot tears, and the light dazzled and I couldn't see clearly. I should have known. I should have recognized him with my heart, if not my eyes. But stupidly I mistook him for one of the men who worked in the gardens there. I stood there, trying to speak, and finally I forced words past the stone in my chest: "He has been taken, please sir, if you know where my dearest one is..." And then, then he said my name—just my name, as I had heard him speak it a thousand times—"Mary." And I knew.

I could tell you more, perhaps, if I could find the words. I might be able to describe how I felt, how he looked, how he sounded, and what he said to me—though I doubt it. We spoke the language of the heart, and of the soul. I find it difficult to translate that into words. He sent me to tell the others. I loved that touch. I, who hadn't been able to say a sensible word, was to be the messenger of the good news that he has risen. It sounds easy, doesn't it? *He has risen.* Try saying it to people whose hopes are in the grave. Try saying it to people who weren't there, who didn't see, didn't feel the touch of his hand, and didn't hear his voice calling their names. He has risen. He has risen.

APPENDIX C

Art Installations for "Driving Away the Dark"

Art within the church, by its very nature, must exist in constant tension between the limitations of a given religious context and the freedom of imagination demanded by artistic expression. It may embellish the worship space, or contrast with it, and it may comfort or unsettle or challenge the worshipers. What we call liturgical art may be purely decorative. True liturgical art may be prophetic, calling us to reach out into previously unexplored territories of the mind and heart. It functions to remind us of the dimensions of sacred time and season. I have created two installations for the women in the gospel of John series, and will do my best to help you envision them—not so you can necessarily reproduce them, but in order to set your own creative imagination free to design something wonderful for your space.

The year we did the series of dramatic monologues we presented a series of objects, symbols of the story being told. We built the basic structure of the art installation on a series of black wire mesh cubes I purchased at an office supply store. This series of square frames comes with round connectors that snap together, enabling you to build a structure of cubes in almost any configuration. To begin, I made seven cubes, and divided them up each Sunday in a different configuration. You can vary the arrangement by turning the cubes in different directions, but always leave the open side toward the congregation. For example, for the first Sunday, Mary at Cana, I had a vertical column of three cubes, and an "L" shaped segment of the remaining four. On top of the vertical column I placed the clear glass decanter of water, and on the cube beneath I placed the pottery pitcher containing the juice. "Mary" took the water and the pitcher to the communion table facing the congregation, to work the "water into wine." For the second Sunday, the Samaritan woman, Mary's water jar and pitcher were in one of the cubes, and there was a large terra-cotta jar located in a cube, placed in the center of the chancel. The "Samaritan woman" was then able to dip her water out as she talked about the living water. In this way, the symbolic items accumulated in the cube structure over the six weeks until either Maundy Thursday or Good Friday. For that special service, we put all the seven cubes with their symbols together in the form of a cross, and placed small votive candles in purple glasses inside each cube. In the darkened sanctuary, the cubes disappear and you see a cross of small, flickering candles dimly lighting the symbols of the women witnesses.[1] On Easter Sunday, we rebuilt the cross out of white wire mesh cubes, put the symbols in, and filled the cubes with white flowers and white votives.

The symbols we used were as follows:

- Mary at Cana: A glass flask of water, a pottery pitcher of juice.
- The Samaritan Woman: A large clay pot of water, and a dipper.
- The Adulteress: A pile of fist-sized stones.
- Martha at Bethany: A length of white cloth, symbolizing a shroud.
- Mary of Bethany: A small white jar with a top.
- Mary at the Cross: A crown of thorns constructed out of grapevine and nails.
- Mary Magdalene: A spray of orchids.

The second time we explored this theme it accompanied a series of six evening lectures and panel discussions on women in the gospels, in the early church, and in the church now. We wanted imagery that would express 2,000 years of darkness and silence. We decided to do a series of painted panels and put them in the chancel, surrounding the worshipers. We constructed six wooden panels, 8' by 2 ¾', and painted them flat black. At the bottom of each, I painted, within a square, an image of the woman witness in color against a gold background. Each week, we hung a panel with the image at about eye level when people were seated. Over the six weeks, the witnesses surrounded the worship space. For Easter we built a cross, 5' by 4', with each panel 2 ¾' wide. It was also painted black, but the cross pieces were covered with painted flowers and branches, symbolizing the four seasons. Mary Magdalene rises up out of the flowers with her arms outstretched to greet the risen Christ who stands at the center. This cross was hung in our baptistry window, at the center back of the raised chancel. We presented the play, "The Women's Tale," on Easter, with low benches and rugs placed in front of the cross. We placed all the elements for communion on a low table in the center, and at the appropriate moment in the play, the women took the elements and served communion to the congregation.

I know this sounds very complex, and perhaps you don't have a painter at your disposal. You could construct something similar out of lighter-weight material, such as black poster board or foam core board, and for the images use color enlargements of artworks depicting the scenes. The important thing is to consider the visual expression as being as important as the spoken word in illuminating the theme.

Notes

[1]I took the big chancel cross down at the beginning of this series, so that the only imagery would be the wire structure. One saint of the church complained that I had banished the cross. I asked her to bear with me, that she would see what I had in mind at the end. When she came to the Good Friday service and saw all the cubes configured into a cross, she said, "Oh! The cross was here all the time; we just didn't recognize it until all the pieces came together." That's a pretty profound description of the gospel of John. Don't you love it when somebody "gets" it?

APPENDIX D

The Women's Tale (A Play)

Gathering

(Set up room with candles, oil lamps and shawls, afghans, carpet, low table, basket, bread, olives, cheese, grapes, chalice, grape juice. Make it look like a home.)

The Women

Mary Magdalene (MM), Martha of Bethany (Martha), Mary the mother of Jesus (MJ), Miriam (the Samaritan woman at the well), Mary of Bethany (MB), Rachel (the woman taken in adultery)

Gathering Chant *(Choose an appropriate hymn)*

MM: I am so glad to welcome all of you into my home to celebrate the Lord's Day. This is a new thing, so I know you'll excuse me if everything isn't quite perfect. We have all celebrated the Sabbath for so long, and the men are having such a hard time getting straight what we should do now.

Martha: Of course, making a lot of work out of something that should be simple. We celebrate the Sabbath Friday to Saturday night, as always, and the Lord's Day on the first day of the week. *The day he rose!*

All: Amen! Hosanna! Alleluia!

Miriam: Well, the men of my village are confused. They want to call the Lord's Day the Sabbath. What will we call Friday night and Saturday?

MB: The first thing, they start making rules!

Rachel: Yes! So which is today, the Sabbath or the Lord's Day?

MM: Today is the Lord's Day, but we are going to combine it with the Sabbath, because we are here to recall the old and look to the new.

MJ: And celebrate both!

MM: We have two purposes, then. The first is to celebrate together. But also there is another reason. As I am sure you have noticed, there are some strange stories going around! Those of us who were here—well, from the beginning, we know what happened. We heard. We saw. We know. But some of the stories I have heard—well, sometimes it's hard to believe they are talking about the same man Jesus we all knew.

Martha: It's a little hard to recognize ourselves!

Miriam: Yes! (*looks at MM*) You'll never believe what I heard them say about you the other day...

MM: Oh, I know, I've heard.

Martha: And I heard someone thinks you are my sister!

MB: And they have me confused with the woman who went to the dinner at Simon's house, and washed the Lord's feet with her tears and dried them with her hair.

Miriam:(*looks at MM*) Wasn't that you?

MM: No, and it wasn't Mary either. At Simon's house, I mean. That was someone else.

Rachel: What was her name?

MM: Mary.

MB: Of course, what else? You'd think our mothers didn't know any other names.

MM: And so, we thought–Mary and Martha and Mary, and well, Mary...

MB: So, do you think there are enough Marys in the room? Thank God for you, Rachel.

MM: We'll try not to get confused! Anyway, we all were thinking that if we got together, and told our stories to each other, and wrote them down, then there would be a record of how it really happened. Because, I think the day will come very soon when our voices will not be so welcome, and our stories may be forgotten–or told from someone else's point of view. So, we will welcome the Sabbath, *and* celebrate the Lord's Day, by telling our stories!

As you see, we have a very special guest with us today. I know you have all seen the Lord's mother, Mary of Nazareth, but perhaps not spoken with her until today (*indicates MJ*).

Miriam: I didn't recognize you without the blue robe!

MJ: Somebody gave me that. I never wear it. It shows the dirt.

MM: So, today, Mary will begin with the Sabbath prayer. Mary, we are so honored...

Sabbath Prayer (*Sung or recited as she lights two candles*)

Barukh atah Adonai Eloheinu, melekh haolam, asher kid'shanu b'mitzvotay v'tzivanu l'hadlik ner shel shabbat

(Blessed are You, Lord our God, King of the universe, who has made us holy through His commandments and commanded us to kindle the Sabbath light.)

MJ: It is good to welcome the Sabbath and the Lord's Day in your house, Mary. And it was such a good idea to invite all our women disciples to share it with us. You know, it is becoming such a public event these days. Of course, I enjoy it when James and Peter are there, but when the men gather, it isn't so easy to talk. Sometimes, I think I'll scream if I can't find someone to just talk.

MM: You're right. It's good to have someone to talk with–someone who understands, who was really there. And you were...right from the beginning.

MJ: Yes, in a way. But really, what was the beginning?

MM: Why...Bethlehem, of course! The stable, the angels caroling "*Hosanna in the highest!*"

MJ: (*laughs*) Oh, *that* beginning: humbled kings and exalted shepherds and a stable by starlight; rumors of angels, angels singing "*Hosanna.*" It was the sound of joy.

MM: It always sounds so wonderful.

MJ: It was. It was also very uncomfortable, like life. Well, that was one beginning. My oldest son always said the real beginning was when Adam and Eve got bored (*they laugh*).

MM: Did he often talk about the old stories? The prophets and kings?

MJ: Oh, yes. He loved to teach. I, of course, was his first pupil (*sighs*). Sons! Why do we want sons so much? They are so aggravating.

MM: You don't really mean that?

MJ: Oh yes. You know, you long for them, and then you have them...not an easy process, as I dare say you know. Then, for the first twelve years of their lives they think you are the sun and moon–the strongest, wisest, most powerful person in the universe. Who do they come to when the world is confusing and demand an explanation? *Mother.* Who do they cry for when they are hurt? *Mother.* Who comforts their fears and holds them close, promising that everything will be all right? And you know, you hold them, and you promise, and you almost believe it yourself, that you can protect them and keep them safe. You have to, or else neither of you would have the courage to send him out the door, into the world, where anything can happen. So where do they learn courage and resolution? Then, one day, they are thirteen and a man. Suddenly you are just a woman, and a mother. Relegated to the corners of their lives.

MM: It never seemed to me that you spent much time in corners.

MJ: Well, perhaps not. So, he taught me. And I listened. Not a bad student, all things considered, *for a woman* (*laughs*).

Mary's Tale: Part I, Cana

Bethlehem *was* wonderful, and the presents were *very* nice, but, you know, it wasn't somehow *real.* It was like being inside a story. It took the pain, and the fear and the cold and the hopes and the blood and turned it all into something exalted and high up and untouchable. I was caught between the very real and the unimaginable. No, for me the real beginning was that wedding in Cana.

I remember clearly how it all happened. But understanding it—well, that came later. We were invited to the wedding, all my children. Jesus had been in Bethany, and I know he had seen his cousin John. John was there, preaching his heart out to the crowds. He was like that: preaching fire on their heads one minute, quenching it in the Jordan the next. Something happened there, between them. I was anxious when he left. I knew—no, I *felt* that something was changing. But he returned in time to go to Cana for the wedding. I remember looking at him, his face so dear and familiar; I thought I knew every mood, every expression. But somehow his face was withdrawn, remote from me. I worried about it, as we traveled. I didn't ask him about it—in spite of reports to the contrary, I do not nag my children! But I worried.

Well, we got to the wedding, and everyone joined the fun. You know how it is at family celebrations: you eat, you talk, you drink a little wine—all right, a lot of wine. The food, it was fine; the mother of that household is a good cook, but the wine—well, it was not so good. Don't misunderstand; it was not so bad, either. So there we were, eating, talking, drinking wine—and I noticed that most of the pitchers of wine were empty. I wasn't snooping, you understand, but family *is* family and God forbid everyone should be shamed by the wine running out in the middle of a wedding! I looked at the servants, meaning just to hint that they should fill up the pitchers before anyone noticed. They fell all over themselves telling me that there wasn't any more wine. Well, I couldn't believe it. No wine! And what they had, not so good to start with. How could this have happened? My family would be disgraced, the young couple shamed before their friends. I looked around, and saw my son Jesus standing nearby, talking with his brothers and friends. I have no idea why I mentioned to him that they were running out of wine. They were kin, and I didn't want them to be embarrassed, I suppose. But really, it wasn't his business to fix it. He looked at me, I remember, and the look on his face… It was exactly the way he used to look before going out into the town on some little errand. I've seen it a thousand times. "I know I am big and strong, and I know I must be about my tasks, but…it really is all right, isn't it? Safe? You will be here when I get back?" Never saying any of it, you understand, but his face *speaking* it? He said something, reminding me that it wasn't his business to interfere. Well—for years, he had been the man of the house, you understand, since Joseph died. I just turned to him as I always did. "They have no wine," I said. Just that. "They have no wine." Then he looked at the water jars standing near by, and I'd seen *that* look before, too. When he'd solved some problem or other, or had decided on just the right way to begin a job of work.

Then—well, he looked at me with eyes that were on fire with something that was not grief or anger or joy or hope or anything else, but rather everything at once, and something more. He stepped back from me, and I could tell he wasn't seeing me, or the empty water jars, or the wedding guests, or anything else that I could see. His eyes–his whole *being*–were fixed on something beyond my sight. He motioned toward the servants. "Do whatever he tells you," I told them. He had them fill the jars–*huge* jars–with water, and I saw the water as it went splashing in. *(Pour a small amount of water from clear jar into pitcher of grape juice.)* I felt my heart shrink inside me. I don't know what I expected–I don't know that I really expected anything. I knew that my son had changed, that my little boy had gone forever, and something wonderful and terrible was going to happen. And I knew that it *had* to happen. The noise of the talking, the dancing–it all faded to silence around me. I could not see anything but those jars of water.

I think my heart stopped.

The servants tipped the jars, and I saw a stream of deep red flowing out, pouring out, spilling out: wine, new wine, wine like blood, rivers of sweet wine. I see it still. *(Pour juice or wine from pitcher into clear chalice on table.)* This wine was not conceived in the belly of a grape.

Rachel: I'd like to share how it was for me, if you'd like to hear?
All: Yes, yes. Tell us. What happened for you?

Rachel's Tale

I remember, when I was very little, that I used to collect stones from the fields near our house. I would build little houses, and lay straw and twigs across to make roofs. My little stone village even had a well in the center–a hole I scooped out of the dust, with stones around it, and I would fill it with water from my mother's big jar in the kitchen. As I worked, I would sing. I sang as I carried the stones; I sang as I built my village; I sang as I carried water. I remember the woman who lived next to us shaking her head as she watched me. I heard her say to my mother, "She lives in a dream world." My mother smiled, and shrugged. "Let her sing and dream, while she may," was all she would say.

Then life changed for me. I was given in marriage, and my husband was not the sort to tolerate dreaming or singing when there was work to be done. I cleaned, cooked, and carried water, and occasionally I helped remove stones from the fields. But there was no music in my work, nor in my life. How can life be full of activity, busy from each moment to the next, yet still be empty? How can there be ceaseless sound–the chatter of voices, the grinding of grain on stone, the snoring of sleepers, the lowing of animals, yet all seem silent? You know what happened. I met a man, and he paid attention to me. He smiled, and he wooed me, and I fell into temptation. Life was empty, without purpose or meaning. What did it matter? I mattered to no one, not even to myself. So I became an adulteress.

My husband must have suspected, for he set watchers, and we were caught. I suppose I did matter to him, when it came to someone else possessing his property. Even after all this time, I can barely bring myself to remember that afternoon. They came crashing into my house, those men, and dragged me out into the street. The shock of them, suddenly there in the room, their rough hands seizing me, forcing me through the door without letting me cover myself, dragging me along the dusty road—it deadened my senses. I remember it seemed dark, though it was mid-day. Voices shouted and howled around me, but I couldn't understand the words. I must have fallen, and been dragged, but at the time I didn't feel the pain. Then they flung me down at the feet of a man seated in the temple, and as I lay there in the dirt, my mind cleared a little. Humiliation greater than the sea flooded me, and I lay there, drowning in it, praying for it to be over soon.

I knew they would kill me. I caught a glimpse of someone stooping for a stone. I wondered, through the sea of shame, how long it would take them to kill me; whether someone would hit me in the head with one of the first stones, killing me quickly, or if it would take all afternoon to die. I heard one of them telling the man, there in temple with everyone listening and looking at me, that I was an adulteress, and asking him if they should stone me to death. I tried to peek up at him, tried to see the face of this man who would judge whether I lived or died. He bent down, and wrote something in the dust. I tried to see what it was, but I was afraid to lift my head. Then I heard him say, "If you have never sinned, then throw your stone." My flesh shrank on my bones, tried to melt into the dust, cringing away from that first cruel pain of striking stone. I couldn't even cry. And we waited, he and I, for the rain of death to fall on me.

But nothing happened. It got quiet; there was no sound at all, except for the sound of stones falling, just falling out of their hands, and then I heard shuffling steps as if people were…*leaving*. He went on writing in the dust, and this time I did lift my head to look into his face. He was looking at me. And more than that, he was *seeing* me. Not just the lonely wife. Not just the adulterous woman. He was seeing *me*: the builder, the singer, the dreamer. "Where are your accusers?" he asked me. I looked around then, and saw…no one. "Does no one accuse you?" he asked. I shook my head then, and managed to whisper, "No one." He smiled then, in that *seeing* way, and said, "Neither do I accuse you. Go now, and sin no more." I stood up, and looked down at the dust where he had been writing. His quick fingers had erased what had been written there, before I could see. But I know what it was, because he wrote the words on my heart, as well as in the dust. He had written forgiveness. He had written mercy. He had written music. He had written my dreams.

Miriam's Tale

He looked tired. That was the first thing I noticed. Tired, and hot, and dusty from the roads. I was looking at him, but I tried not to let him see that I was looking at him. It was the sixth hour, and the sun was cruelly hot. It was always hot when I went to the well for water. I could not go when the other women went, in the morning. I would see them, from my doorway, all in a bunch, talking and jabbering and laughing as they went to draw water from Jacob's well. They would draw aside from my door when they passed, and they would not look at me. It was nonsense, what they talked, such foolish nonsense those women talked. I would stand there, in the shadow cast by the door, and listen to them, peek out at them, and my heart would bleed with longing to be with them, to be included in all that foolish talk, to be one of them. Oh, I must have cried enough water to fill a well, for all the good it did me. There was not enough water in the wide world to wash me clean enough for them. Well, so there I was, in the heat of the day, and there he was, and I could see he was a Jew. So I was careful, because even though I was not respectable, I didn't want him to insult me or—or even spit on me. You think sometimes there is nothing else that can shame you, and then—someone thinks of a way.

I drew my shawl around me, and tried to make myself small inside it. I came near the well, and I was reaching down to draw the water when—and I'll never forget it because I nearly died of the shock—he spoke to me. In broad daylight! He asked me for a drink. I looked around to see who he was talking to. I only had the one dipper, and I knew he wouldn't dream of drinking out of it. I said something idiotic; I asked him what was he thinking! Did he propose to put his lips where my unclean, Samaritan lips had rested? I was afraid. My throat was so dry I could hardly force the words past my lips. Then he smiled at me. Have you any idea how long it had been since anyone had smiled at me? And then he said that if I knew who I was talking to, I would have asked *him* for a drink, and that he would give me water that was *alive.*

I stood there, in that cruel hot sun, my throat aching, my eyes dry from too many tears shed, and he talked about water that was alive. "Well," I managed to say, "the well is about a hundred feet deep, and you don't seem to have a dipper. Where is this living water?" Then he answered me. That's all. It may not sound like much, now. He listened to me, and he answered me. We talked together, he and I. About me, my lonely, wasted life—too many men and not one love, and about God. And somehow God didn't feel so remote, up there on his holy mountain, or in Jerusalem, depending on who you're talking to. God seemed—there. I knew, then. I don't know how, but I knew. "I know that Messiah is coming," I told him. I looked into his eyes and he smiled again. "I am," he said. That's all. "I am." And I knew it was the truth—the truth that poured out around me like a fountain in the desert, like a river, like a never-ending stream. So I put down my jug and I ran back to my village—because, when you have found something so wonderful as water that is alive, well…you want to share it, don't you? And you know, they listened to me, and they went to see and hear him. *They listened to me!* I still have to go to Jacob's well for everyday water. But now I go with the others. And we all talk—silly, nonsense talk—and laugh.

Sometimes, we talk about that other water, that spring in what was the desert of our souls, that water that is *alive!*

Martha's Tale

You know how it is that you can love someone, and still be so mad at that person you can hardly bear it? It was like that for me, that day when I saw Jesus coming up the road. I thought about how my brother had lain in his sick bed, calling for Jesus. Not because he wanted a miracle, mind you. Lazarus would never think of asking anything for himself. No, he just wanted to see his dear friend one last time. I remember my sister looking at me, across his sick bed, her eyes dark with sorrow, asking, asking…, "Why doesn't he come?" We waited, and our brother grew weaker, and finally he stopped calling, stopped looking toward the window, stopped…breathing. I couldn't believe it! Jesus had not come, had sent no word, nothing. All those others he had healed, comforted, and not one word for us, for his friend Lazarus whom he loved. I had gone out of the house, unable to look at my sister any longer. She just sat there, not moving, not speaking, not crying—frozen with pain, disappointment, and grief. Mary—well, she takes things so to heart, even little things. I've seen her cry her eyes out over a dead bird, or a lamb born too soon, too weak to live. And she was never one to go near people; I couldn't believe my eyes when she started to creep into the room and listen to Jesus when he came. After that, she just lived for those times when Jesus would come, and she could sit at his feet and listen to what he said. Still as a mouse, she would listen as if her life depended upon it. Oh, I can be a little impatient with her; I know it. It's a beautiful thing to see a young person lit up with joy, living in a world of the spirit. But it's one less pair of hands to make the bread and wash the clothes. It's fine to talk about the bread of life, but between us, there had also better be bread on the table when everyone's hungry from all that talking! That's the difference between us. I live in *this* world. I've baked many a loaf of bread for Jesus, and given him room in my house to sleep, and taken care that he knew he was loved! And when my brother needed him, I wanted him to come! I trusted him to come. But he didn't.

Then, when Lazarus died and had been buried in the tomb, *then* I saw Jesus coming up the road toward my house. I was filled with pure rage! I wanted to shake him, scream at him, and tell him how he had failed us. How he had failed my brother, who only wanted to see him one more time, hear the sound of his voice, or touch his hand. Was it so much to ask, I wondered? So, before I knew it, I was running, running toward him, shaking my fist in the air, and crying. I don't do that often, you know. I'm usually the one everyone runs to when they are in trouble. I'm called on to be strong, to take charge. How many tears have soaked into these shoulders, I wonder, as I soothed and patted and assured someone who was crying out their woes in my arms? Well, this time I didn't feel strong, and I didn't feel calm, and there was no one there to hold or comfort me.

He stopped, and waited for me. Then, in the midst of all that rage and yelling and crying, I stopped, too. He was looking at me, and I knew that he had the power to make everything all right. I don't know how I knew. Miracle stories are fine when they are about someone else. But my brother was dead, dead and buried and gone, and yet here I was, certain that Jesus could somehow make it all right. I didn't even dare to put it into words. All I could say was, "If you had been here, my brother would not have died. And if you ask God for something, anything, God will give it to you." He stood there in the road, with the sun all around him, and the look of pure love shining out of his eyes, and tears, too: tears for my brother, for my sister, for me. And I knew that everything would be all right. And then he asked me if I believed that Lazarus would rise again. Now, the teachers have told us for a long time that the righteous will rise on the last day. And surely my brother was righteous. So I said yes, I knew he would rise on the last day. But that was not what I wanted, and Jesus knew it. I wanted life for my brother, life here and now! I know it was unreasonable; I know it was selfish. But I wanted my brother to live! Then Jesus talked to me, in the way he had talked to others in my house, many times. But this time I was not too busy to listen. I heard his words, and they wrote themselves on my heart in letters of fire that have never gone out. "I am the resurrection and the life. If you believe in me, even if you are dead, you shall live. And everyone who lives and believes in me shall never die."

Now I'm not saying I understood everything, all at once. We went to the tomb, and when he asked me to roll the stone away, I was confused and frightened. First of all, I could not roll away that great stone. And I was afraid of what lay on the other side. I didn't understand, but somehow…I believed. Mary says that is the greatest part of his teaching. When Jesus speaks to you, it writes words of fire on your heart, and you believe. And believing, you shall never die. So we rolled the stone away and faced death. And you know what happened. Death became life. We didn't know that day, as we saw Lazarus come out of the tomb, that soon, too soon, we would stand at another tomb, and weep. But we should have known That no tomb could hold him, no stone separate him from us. I still live in this world, with my brother and sister. We live, and we shall die. But I know, because the words still burn on my heart, that, when we do at last die, Jesus will be there, rolling the stone away.

Mary's Tale: Part II, Golgotha

They tell me it was dark. I had no vision to spare for the sky. I stood there, not alone, yet more alone than I shall ever be again. Those who also loved him best were there, with me, but I have no memory of their faces or their tears. I have no memory of their loving arms as they sheltered me against the enormity of loss and held me up when bone and muscle would have crumpled and failed. I have no memory of their voices, soft and shaken. Now their voices sing me to sleep, voices of comfort, and of hope. Now their voices speak out boldly, powerfully of the message of the Messiah. They are my sisters and daughters, inheritors of the good news.

But I do not remember them there, in that place. I remember only the face and the voice of my son. And I remember the pain.

There, in that place, the entire world became pain. I breathed it, I writhed under it, it crushed my heart, and it was all I could do to hold on. But, you see, it might be that my presence there comforted him a little–the way I comforted him when he was little, and hurt or frightened, before the great vision took him and left him so little room for fear–or, rather, made it irrelevant. Nothing could take away the agony he suffered, but just in case my being there, loving him... Well, I *had* to be there.

I have other children. I have sons and daughters, who look to me to be strong and continually faithful. They seem to think it important that I be here, still part of the story that continues to unfold. I tell them, "We are at only the very beginning of the journey, you and I." I am not comfortable when some of them want to set me apart, as if I were somehow not quite human. They don't understand that *that* is the most wonderful part of this journey we are on to make God's kingdom real. The vision is vested in us, the real, ordinary people who live, love, and die as people have for thousands of years, and will go on doing until the end. Do not make me out to be more than I am, I say. For what I am is quite enough. I am a woman who had a child. That child was filled up with God in a way the world has never seen and shall never see again. He embodied God. And God summoned me to be one of his disciples, so that all women everywhere would see that the kingdom is theirs, too.

I cannot speak about the day he died. And, you know, my son came among us to teach us all how to live. That is what I remember. And so should you.

Mary Magdalene's Tale: Part I, the Healing

I remember the beginning for me. It's so vivid I can't always tell the *then* from the *now*. My life before was so...terrible. Oh, I know what people say of me, but the plain truth is that I had been the victim of a terrible illness. My mind was dark, darker than any desert night, and the demons possessed me. I can remember only enough of what it was like to be unwilling to remember more. The most terrible part was that a tiny corner of my mind remained my own, aware. Oh yes, I was aware of the stares, the whispers, the pity and fear. I was aware of the coming of the demons. Then the darkness would take me, and my body would become a battleground for them, screeching, clamoring for possession. I never knew when it would seize me—in the middle of a meal, or as I walked to the well with the other women, or as I was talking with a friend.

I would be so...ashamed. People were afraid, you know. They whispered that I must be a terrible sinner, to be so afflicted. No man would marry me, of course. No dowry was big enough to overcome my illness. Demons, they called it. People would hurry their children indoors when I passed—as if I might, you know, hurt them. I don't know how I stood it, all those years. Then, he took it all from me: the demons, the pain, the shame, and the terrible sense of guilt. My tiny mind-self would pray for God to release me in death. Instead, God released me to life. You take so much for granted, you who have never been owned by demons: the smell of morning; the sound of birds singing, chattering; the warmth of the sun; the shining mystery of the moon; the touch of someone's hand, strong and comforting, driving away the dark. He gave me all that. And I stopped wanting anything in the world except to be near him, to help him, to love him. Just to hear the sound of his voice. I was born that day. I'll love him until I die. If only I could have died for him. I only wish we could have had...just a little more time. But he would go to Jerusalem. He *would* go. But first he went back to Bethany.

Mary of Bethany's Tale

I know others remember the other supper, the last one. But I remember that dinner table in my sister's house, before everything ended, and began again. I remember the smell of the flowering almond tree outside the window, all the world fresh with the smell of evening rain: life coming back to the dead land, the promise of spring, and the unbearable sweetness of life. He sat at the table, and talked. Martha had prepared a special meal, and if you have ever eaten at Martha's table, you know that *that* is special indeed. Everything must be just so, just right. It wasn't the Sabbath, just a meal, but for him, well, every day was a celebration of life. But I saw the end in his face. I remember looking at him and thinking, "Oh God, not yet, not yet!" But his eyes told me everything. He had taught us about letting go of things, of not letting anything possess us—not even your own life. In his eyes I saw that he was letting go of everything he loved, all of us, all except God. I looked around, wondering why none of them spoke about it, why Peter didn't jump up and down and tell him not to think like that, things were just getting going, no time to be talking about the end—but he didn't. He didn't understand. He didn't see. None of them saw. Except me.

I've never been able to do things like other people. I'm not that good a cook. And I have never wanted to marry. People can't understand that. They say that's all daughters are good for—to marry and have children. I used to cry myself to sleep when I thought about leaving home, going to someone else's house, being someone's wife. I couldn't bear it. I know you all think Martha is bossy. Well, she is. But she always understood how it was with me. She used to say, "Never mind, little mouse. You shall stay at home and be my joy." I know I make her impatient sometimes, but she always let me stay at home where I wanted to be. Then Jesus came. And I didn't feel helpless and stupid any more. I understood that it was my part to listen, and to understand.

So I understood that we had come to the end. And I wondered what I could do for him, anything to show how much I loved him and thanked him for loving me. We put sweet spices and herbs on the dead. What do we do to perfume the life of the living? I got the nard we had bought and saved, and I anointed his feet with it, and he smiled at me. Martha understood. The others were angry–such *expense*. Some of them–well, they never understood that we were to have him for just a little while. I had heard about the gifts from the visitors when he was born: frankincense and myrrh. It seemed–well, his life was the fragrance of hope for everyone who knew him–so it just seemed…*right* to give him the sweetness of spring to remember us by. I poured it out and the fragrance filled the room.

MJ: I begged him not to go into Jerusalem. Well, it wasn't the first time I had tried to warn him. "Don't you know," I asked him, "what will happen if you keep challenging the authorities?" Throwing the moneylenders out of the temple. "What did you think you were doing?" I asked him. "Kicking them where it hurts," he said, "in the wallet." Well, how long did he suppose he could go around breaking the laws?

Miriam: Some of them were really stupid laws. I've always thought so.

MJ: I know. I know he was *right,* but I wanted him to be *safe!* Anyway, he didn't listen. Couldn't, I suppose. Once he walked through that door he couldn't go back. Couldn't be my little boy any more. But that didn't mean I had to keep quiet about it, then or now. It's easy to believe when you watch a miracle. Then, time passes, and people think, "Well, that was nice…but what are you going to do for me today?"

MM: Lazarus, at any rate, stayed faithful. Of course, he could hardly do otherwise. Being raised from the dead, and all.

MJ: Yes. (*looks at Martha and Mary of Bethany*) And his sisters may have had something to do with *that.* My dears, I know you will always be true friends. But in the face of personal danger, it's quite easy to become forgetful. Think of all those people in Jerusalem. I remember how they screamed and cried, laughed and danced and sang. Here he came, riding on that colt. How he did love Isaiah.

Martha: Why did he do that? Why, when he knew it was so dangerous. He could have walked into the city; he was almost there. But he sent for that poor animal to ride on. To deliberately…well, flaunt the prophecy like that.

MJ: I think he did it so people would have to really examine their beliefs. It's one thing to believe in a prophecy. There is something so satisfying about the old stories...the Messiah, so longed for, King of Zion, to come riding on an ass's colt. I don't think anyone ever really examined that passage for the *truth* of it. In real life, kings come in chariots, behind horses, with all the trimmings. They don't come humble and accompanied by a ragged band of followers, riding on an ass like a peasant. Well, kings are supposed to have power: power to throw out the Romans; power to reestablish the land of the covenant, to rebuild what has been thrown down. *Wealth. Influence. Pride.* They took one look at my son, and they saw none of that.

MB: But there was such joy! They did recognize him, we all thought so!

MJ: Oh, yes. *Then.* They cried "Hosanna" that day, too, just like the angels. But they meant something different by it. The angels sang praise to God. But the people? They wanted something. "Save us now," that's what they meant by Hosanna. (*whispers*) *"Save us."* Lord, some of them even tore off their clothes and capered about. Their mothers would have died of shame and I told them so! Not that they listened. The city had gone mad. You could hear the stories in the streets, all about Lazarus and the great miracle. Proof that he was the Messiah. The King was coming.

Miriam: Some people didn't believe it, about Lazarus.

Martha: Yes, but there were a lot of people who had seen Lazarus come out of the tomb. They testified all over the city.

MM: I don't suppose they knew they were condemning him.

MJ: Not then, no. But later. Oh, they blamed it on the government, of course. It was Rome's fault. It was the Sanhedrin's fault. People can always find someone to blame when they need to. And Pilate! The man is so wishy-washy I'm surprised he could decide which hand to wash first. Oh yes, they collected their evidence, the leaders, and questioned all those who had been cleansed or healed or just merely impressed, and then they condemned him. But Pilate gave the people a choice. He asked them, "Barabbas or Jesus?" They chose Barabbas, a murderer, a man who took life. And my son had done nothing but give life. In the end it all came down to that: a choice. And the people—not the government, not the politicians, not the religious hierarchy—the people chose. And they chose Barabbas and let my son die.

MB: Why? Oh, why did they do it? The same people had shouted "*Hosanna!*" just days before, and they were sincere then—at least, many of them were. Why did they choose Barabbas?

MJ: When my son came into the city he held up their beliefs to them, like a mirror: "You have asked for a Messiah, and here he is, just as the prophecy says: a man, poor and humble." They wanted a king. They got a suffering servant. What good is that to a people who want someone else to fix all their problems? They were poor, desperate, afraid. I think, there in the face of Rome, they wanted *Hosanna,* to be saved. And then they looked at my son the carpenter, and remembered that donkey.

Rachel: Remember, there is the rest of the story. (*nods to MM*)

MJ: Yes. I do remember. I'm so glad you are all here, listening. I find it difficult to talk about all this to anyone who wasn't really there. I have to be brave all the time, and look always patient and serene.

MM: (*laughs*) Well, you don't...always! Neither do I.

MJ: No, we are uppity women who speak the truth. Well...we must break the bread. It's almost time...(*starts to rise*)

Martha: (*interrupts her with a gesture*) Mary—that day in Jerusalem, did you know what would happen?

MJ: No. But I was afraid. The man of peace is always at the mercy of the violent. Nothing is more dangerous than the truth. Nothing is so fleeting as popular opinion. But he came, and everyone cheered, and, for a moment, I think we all saw the truth...whole and clear and undeniable. Just for a moment...perfect truth.

MM: What did you do?

MJ: What everyone else did. I cried "*Hosanna!*"

Miriam: Let's pray together the things that are on our hearts. Everyone, let us pray.

Prayers of the Gathered Community

Hymn

Communion

(*MM picks up one of the baskets of bread.*)

Martha: Let me help with that...(*attempts to rise and reaches for the basket*)

MM: Just sit. Always you're helping, always you're busy. Today you're a guest. So sit. Mary (*looks at Mary of Bethany*), you help (*hands her the wine*). (*Miriam and Mary of Nazareth go forward to help also*)

(*The women pass the bread and wine and invite everyone to share, saying,* "The Body of Jesus given for you," *and,* "The cup of salvation poured out for you.")

Mary Magdalene's Tale: Part II, the Garden

So you want to know how it was, that early morning when I went to grieve over the body of my Lord? It was quiet, and the cold and darkness of night lingered among the stones and trees. No bird sang. No small huddled creatures made a sound. I was alone as I had never been, not even in my illness. I had left his mother at last and come alone to the tomb. I thought it might comfort her to know that I had been there, although I couldn't go in and tend to him because of the stone. They had sealed the tomb, you see, because they were afraid someone would steal him away. So I knew I couldn't go in, couldn't even clean his wounds or lay a few flowers on his breast. It was pointless, really, going there, but something drew me and I couldn't resist. I walked up the slope, and I felt as if my body was made of stone. My eyes were dry as dust, dry as death. My heart felt like a stone, filling my chest, crowding out the air, because—*the stone was rolled away.*

I stood there, like a fool, staring without seeing, without understanding. The stone was rolled away. I stooped and looked in, but—even now I cannot make my lips to shape the words. I fell down then, and all I could think was, "They've taken his poor body, broken and dishonored, they've robbed us of even his bones to mourn over." I know that others came then, Peter and John, drawn there as I was, and then they ran off again. But I couldn't move, couldn't make sense of anything. It was as if the darkness possessed me again, as if the demons had returned. Finally, I stood up and turned to go. And there was this man standing there. My eyes, dry for so many hours, were suddenly filled with tears, hot tears, and the light dazzled and I couldn't see clearly. I should have known. I should have recognized him with my heart, if not my eyes. But stupidly I mistook him for one of the men who worked in the gardens there. I stood there, trying to speak, and finally I forced words past the stone in my chest: "He has been taken, please sir, if you know where my dearest one is…" And then, then he said my name—just my name, as I had heard him speak it a thousand times—"Mary." And I knew.

I could tell you more, perhaps, if I could find the words. I might be able to describe how I felt, how he looked, how he sounded, and what he said to me—though I doubt it. We spoke the language of the heart, and of the soul. I find it difficult to translate that into words. He sent me to tell the others. I loved that touch. I, who hadn't been able to say a sensible word, was to be the messenger of the good news that he has risen. It sounds easy, doesn't it? He has risen. Try saying it to people whose hopes are in the grave. Try saying it to people who weren't there, who didn't see, didn't feel the touch of his hand, and didn't hear his voice calling their names. He has risen. He has risen.

ALL: Hosanna! Alleluia! Amen!

Bibliography

Barclay, William. *Introduction to John and the Acts of the Apostles.* Philadelphia: Westminster Press, 1976.

Borg, Marcus J. *The God We Never Knew: Beyond Dogmatic Religion to a More Authentic Contemporary Faith.* New York: HarperCollins, 1997.

Brown, Raymond E. *The Community of the Beloved Disciple: The Life, Loves, and Hates of an Individual Church in New Testament Times.* New York: Paulist Press, 1979.

_____, *The Gospel According to John.* 2 vols. Anchor Bible. Garden City, N.Y.: Doubleday, 1966, 1970.

_____, "Roles of Women in the Fourth Gospel." Appendix 2 in *The Community of the Beloved Disciple: The Life, Loves, and Hates of an Individual Church in New Testament Times.* New York: Paulist Press, 1979.

Crossan, John Dominic. *The Historical Jesus: The Life of a Mediterranean Jewish Peasant.* San Francisco: HarperSanFrancisco, 1991.

De Boer, Esther. *Mary Magdalene: Beyond the Myth.* Harrisburg, Pa.: Trinity Press International, 1997.

Frankel, Ellen. *The Five Books of Miriam: A Woman's Commentary on the Torah.* San Francisco: HarperSanFrancisco, 1996.

Haskins, Susan. *Mary Magdalen: Myth and Metaphor.* New York: Riverhead Books, 1993.

King, Karen L. *The Gospel of Mary of Magdala: Jesus and the First Woman Apostle.* Santa Rosa, California: Polebridge Press, 2003.

Marjanen, Antti. *The Woman Jesus Loved: Mary Magdalene in the Nag Hammadi Library and Related Documents.* Nag Hammadi and Manichaean Studies. Leiden/New York/Cologne: E.J. Brill, 1996.

McKenna, Megan. *Leave Her Alone.* Maryknoll, N.Y.: Orbis Books, 2000.

Pagels, Elaine H. *Beyond Belief: The Secret Gospel of Thomas.* New York: Random House, 2003.

Reid, Barbara. *Choosing the Better Part?: Women in the Gospel of Luke.* Collegeville, Minn.: Liturgical Press, 1996.

Russell, Letty M., ed. *Feminist Interpretation of the Bible.* Philadelphia: Westminster Press, 1985.

Schaberg, Jane. *The Resurrection of Mary Magdalene: Legends, Apocrypha, and the Christian Testament.* New York: Continuum, 2003.

Schneiders, Sandra M. *Written That You May Believe: Encountering Jesus in the Fourth Gospel.* New York: Crossroad, 1999.

Schüssler Fiorenza, Elisabeth. *Discipleship of Equals: A Critical Feminist Ecclesiology (Ekklesia-logy) of Liberation.* New York: Crossroad, 1994.

_____. "A Feminist Critical Interpretation for Liberation: Martha and Mary: Lk. 10:38–42." *Religion and Intellectual Life* 3 (1986).

_____. *In Memory of Her: A Feminist Theological Reconstruction of Christian Origins.* New York: Crossroad, 1983.

Sloyan, Gerard S. *John. Interpretation: A Bible Commentary for Teaching and Preaching.* Atlanta: John Knox Press, 1988.

Trible, Phyllis. "Feminist Hermeneutics and Biblical Studies." *Christian Century* 99 (1982).